# FREEDOM BRIDGE

# FREEDOM BRIDGE:

# MARYKNOLL IN HONG KONG

## by Bill Surface and Jim Hart

COWARD-McCANN, Inc.   New York

# ACKNOWLEDGMENTS

*Several Maryknoll Fathers do not emerge as leading characters, but have contributed to this book. Thanks goes to Fathers Thomas Bauer, William Downs, James E. McDermott and Albert Nevins of Maryknoll, and to Jack Geoghegan, Ellis Amburn, Betsy Cullen and Richard Schultz.*

# CONTENTS

*Illustrations follow page 96.*

# FREEDOM BRIDGE

# 1.

## INTO THE LABYRINTH

FOR uncounted millions the choice was one of three: to be liquidated, become slave labor or volunteer for suicidal war teams in Korea. It was 1950 and the Communists had defeated the Chinese Nationalists.

One small, assorted million—peasants, intellectuals, artisans, doctors, politicians—did escape via the Canton-Hong Kong railway. They carried their little packs of personal belongings over the 50-foot wooden bridge at Lowu, trudged into the Kowloon section of the British Crown Colony of Hong Kong, and walked into an even greater confusion.

There was no room in Kowloon. There was none across the harbor on Hong Kong Island. Some climbed hitherto unusable hillsides and dug caves or built homes of cardboard boxes, flattened tin cans and tar paper. Others hovered in doorways and on rooftops or slept on sidewalks with rice sacks as blankets. Death took a steady toll nightly, and a special sanitary squad went on a regular schedule removing the bodies.

The already cramped colony—the world's most densely populated area with its census total of 600,000—not only reached an automatic saturation point but was near suffocation. Now Hong Kong contained 3,000,000 people and was the world's largest dumping ground.

The government sympathized with, but also ignored, the refugees' appalling existence. After all, officials apologetically maintained, exiled Chinese have great emotional identification with their country and have always returned to their homes following every crisis.

One group of American refugees which fled China—the Maryknoll Fathers [1]—realized that the Hong Kong government's assessment of the refugee condition as temporary was indeed erroneous. Maryknoll, probably more than most missions, was suited to help Chinese refugees. It had entered China in 1918, only shortly after America itself had ceased to be a mission field. Missionary life in the Orient at that time was staid and governed by a strict social code that demanded a businesslike association between religious worker and parishioner. But Maryknoll pioneers had a new approach. These priests slept and ate with peasants, showed them how to prevent disease, how to control flash floods—how to become Christians. The method scandalized some missionaries,

---

[1] Official name: The Catholic Foreign Mission Society of America. Its headquarters are near Ossining, N. Y.

but the Chinese—the people who mattered—called the Maryknoller "Brother." The program revolutionized missionary
techniques and gave new meaning to American ingenuity.

Despite civil wars, large bandit raids and World War II,
Maryknoll Fathers began schools, hospitals, clinics, orphanages, leper colonies, farming cooperatives, seminaries and
churches. Over 300 Maryknoll missionaries were engaged in
the program when the Communists gained complete control
of China and thirty-one years of mission work ended almost
instantly. Communist cadres, which had fashioned themselves along the same lines of Maryknoll's social ideas, intensified campaigns to discredit all religious organizations. Particularly American ones.

Chinese Communist leader Mao Tse-tung publicly divided
the world into "The People" and "The Enemy," and Christians were the enemy. And the legendary Roman Colosseum
perhaps never witnessed such diversity of religious cruelty as
that which followed the Communist victory in China. Those
who thought they knew the full history of man's villainies
realized that this was probably the most heroic story of Christians since the days of Diocletian and Nero.[2]

Missioners, especially in Northern China, were known to
have been undressed, given kangaroo trials, then buried or
boiled alive or stomped to death for their "crimes." Catechists
were rolled in beds of broken glass, or pushed into river ice
holes until they were drowned or frozen. Seminary students

[2] All Maryknoll personnel in China were interviewed by Father Thomas J.
Bauer of Maryknoll for church records and the accounts which have been used
here.

near Peking were nailed hand and foot to two-wheeled carts pulled by horses which were lashed into full gallop over rough roads. Then the executioners slit the boys' chests and cut out their hearts, which they strung on reeds for exhibition. At least one entire Christian village was massacred; one young boy was forced to watch a professional hide-tanner skin his father alive. Other village patriarchs were stripped and forced to climb spike-studded poles until they were torn. The Trappist Monks were taken on a death march in the snowy Manchurian Mountains, with only 44 survivors from the original group of 75 monks and brothers.

By the time the Communist army reached Maryknoll's South China territory, Red tactics had been overhauled. In late 1948, the Communist Politburo—perhaps acting upon Russian warning of possible religious uprisings—announced: "Make no more public martyrs." Thereupon the Communists became more subtle. With clocklike precision, pain and pleasure were administered until victims reacted to such stimuli with animal obedience. This refined cruelty—they called it "Washing the brain"—left no visible marks other than glazed eyes and haggard faces. In time the victims would slip into deep shock and do what they were told or go mad or die of "natural" causes.

When expelled missionaries reached the Hong Kong side of Lowu Bridge, their minds held many scars. A French priest kept screaming that the Communists were trying to get him into a barber chair to cut his throat; his hair hung down to his shoulders. Some priests had been forced to sit facing white walls or burning lights for months. Nearly all still heard yelling Communist voices.

Although there was a rotating seven-man reception team called the "Border Patrol" to meet religious personnel, the man who became known as the "Border Patrol Priest" was not a member of this group. He was a happy, excitable, bearded little Italian missioner named Ambrose Poletti. He lived only five minutes away by motor scooter, and never missed a day at the border.

Father Poletti is best qualified to describe the scene there:

> The priests—all religions—arrive at border. I meet them, get them passports, show where to go. Most of them are physical, mental wrecks, in rags, starving and pitiful. They crying, out of their mind, still scared Communists after them. Have pistol-butt scars and been whip with chains. They ashamed. Been treated worst than dog. I give them things to drink and eat, but they had been in jail so long they sometimes think I up to trick. I tell them, "All right, you hear, all right now. Now understand, all bad is gone. You free now."
>
> There was ninety-two-year-old French nun. Spend sixty-two years in China helping kids, and she go blind but remember catechism anyway and stay there teaching and helping. Communist tells people in newspaper she kill kids with poison, so they stone her when she leave.
>
> Others like Bishop Alphonse Ferronie. He used to weigh hundred and eighty pounds. Now he weighs seventy pounds. I had to carry like baby, feed like baby. He too weak to eat or hold cup. He come out same day as forty-one American flyers shot down in Korea. He didn't look like human. Nobody know him. Nobody could talk to him. I speak in English and no answer. I speak in French and he not pay attention. Then I speak in Latin and his face turn on like light.

Many of the deported missioners were taken to hospitals. The majority, however, were still strong enough to walk from the railway station to the nearby outdoor restaurant under the trees. They sat at the greasy oilcloth tables with coke, lemonade or beer. Some stared at the tables. Some stared back at the China hills. All regretted being forced to abandon their Christians.

But Maryknoll was in Hong Kong now and determined to rebuild its shattered organization. It wanted to alleviate at least some of the suffering there by giving refugees a new start, helping them find food and jobs, build homes, receive medical care and education for their children. But even charity is sometimes circumscribed, and Maryknoll could not intervene at this particular period. Like twenty-one other Catholic foreign mission societies, it was now a guest of the Italian Milan Fathers who had charge of the Hong Kong district.

# 2.

## ONE OF THE LAST TO LEAVE

THE constant flight of planes overhead was his only contact with the outside world. The athletic-looking young priest from Cambridge, Massachusetts, watched them from his remote To Pong station in the South China mountains. They must mean that Chiang Kai-shek's Nationalists were evacuating the mainland. It was nearly winter in 1949. The priest was Father Stephen B. Edmonds.

His suspense ended at 4 P.M. the day after Thanksgiving, when a young student dashed into the Maryknoll school yelling, "Communists! Communists!"

Father Edmonds went outside. On the whitewashed compound walls were the freshly scrawled words: "Down With Americans!" "Down With Imperialism!" "Men and Women Are Equal," and ironically, "Freedom of Religion for All."

It was the prelude to a prolonged Chinese Communist harassment. Its unpredictable tempo of alternate pressure and easement was sinister; its effect was ravaging.

Preoccupied with Nationalist guerrilla fighting, the Communists ignored the mission until December 23, when a menacing wave of 200 soldiers, speaking an unfamiliar Mandarin dialect, tramped into the compound. They searched for machine guns and remained for two days. In the next four months both disciplined and rowdy Communist soldiers surged in and out of the mission. Guerrilla battles raged around the area, and the Communists would send out false alarms, prompting the local people to take their few possessions and lead their pigs and cows into the mountains. They would return in a couple of days. A week later the performance would be repeated.

Shortly after Easter, Father Edmonds went to the Sz Wong parish to return a visit of some Maryknoll priests. En route he was abruptly halted by a small band of Communist soldiers who seemed astonished at seeing a foreigner. They forced him down the road at gunpoint until they met another Communist patrol. One of these officers spoke Cantonese, surprisingly shook hands with the priest, and quickly arranged for his release and return to To Pong.

Chaos was waiting there. The mission had been taken over by the Communists, who were firing over its walls at Nationalist guerrillas. Father Edmonds ran into the schoolroom and found Father Anthony Karlovecius, his assistant, keeping the children stretched out on the floor.

Father Edmonds went to the top officer and insisted that

they leave. The officer appeared stunned that anyone would order him around while he carried a gun, but left. An hour later, however, the Communists moved mortar and machine guns back to the village.

A Communist leader asked for permission to remain. Father Edmonds showed a letter forbidding either army from using the mission. The cadre said he respected the document, but that this was such an important asssignment he must nullify the order for the "safety of the country." Whereupon the children were herded into the chapel and questioned. Most began crying when the bullets fired by retreating guerrillas hit the roof; their fears were increased when the soldiers bragged about "these men killed." The children knew some of the victims had been their fathers and brothers. One lanky soldier sniggered about quartering a peasant and throwing his body to dogs. The victim's nine-year-old daughter was in the room.

Every time the children began to eat, a Red guard warned them that they were being poisoned. They finally ate their rice at 10 A.M., lying on their stomachs. Father Edmonds could look out his window and see that it was too dangerous for them to sit up; the Communists were readying an attack fifty yards away, and the Nationalist guerrillas were waiting on the other side. But the guerrillas' lack of training, equipment and organization finally forced them to retreat.

The Communists came into the mission and seized a sick, hobbling seventy-six-year-old man as their "guide through the mountains after the enemy." Both priests rushed out and argued against it. While Father Edmonds declaimed loudly, Father Karlovecius quietly led the old man away.

Next morning six armed soldiers strolled into Father Karlovecius' class and ordered the students to stand. The priest told them to sit down. The Communists waved their guns and led the boys off to shell rice for the soldiers. The missioners went to the Communist officer, a bullnecked North Chinese, and told about the intrusion. He laughed for five minutes, while the soldiers even rolled on the floor.

"Yes," the officer said, "troublemakers and bandits should be locked up." Then he ordered his men to jail the two priests. Later the Communists realized that they had been warned against damaging their international prestige by killing religious workers, and the two priests were released.

Returning home, Father Edmonds met an old man holding a machine gun, like a baby. He and other remnants of the Nationalist guerrillas had driven a few Communists out.

"Did you see it, Father, did you see it? See how we beat the Communists? You think with the American help we can drive the bandits out of all China? Do you, do you?"

Father Edmonds didn't answer him. The old man, however, was partially right. The guerrillas courageously drove out the Communists, terminating enemy occupation in the mission. They fought in a heavy rain, chasing the Reds three on three, two on two, and so forth until they killed every one.

Many villagers—now so poor they dug up fresh Communist graves for clothing—returned to their homes, but the fear that the Communists might have a huge army nearby was a real one. Still, the guerrillas were encouraged by news that supplies from Formosa would be air-dropped to them soon, and they fought on.

During the next two months—May and June—the guerrillas and Reds chased each other back and forth. Occasionally wounded guerrillas slipped into the mission for treatment, but Father Edmonds cautioned that this endangered the children's lives. He had no choice with the Communists. Some of them were polite, ate their food, and left promptly. A half hour later a vicious group would barge in and terrorize everyone.

The mission was quiet during July as school ended. Most of the students asked permission to remain an extra week for what they considered their "last schooling." The rest of the summer was relatively uneventful. The area was even quieter in September, when school was supposed to reopen, but Father Edmonds faced two obstacles. He had no funds, and a Communist cadre delivered a written order forbidding the school's reopening. Nevertheless it was opened on October 1. The children had grisly tales of Communist barbarism—such as their playmates being strung from trees by toes and thumbs.

The Communists ignored the mission completely all fall. The priests ventured out for missionary trips, held small instruction meetings, gave medicine and pulled teeth. As December approached they were confident enough to hold a three-week retreat and stage a Christmas play. The boys, however, slept in their clothes in order to escape if Communists did return.

Everyone realized it was only borrowed time. Many fifteen- and sixteen-year-olds asked the priests to marry them before it was too late. A series of To Pong weddings began on January 2, and nearly a hundred Nationalist soldiers slipped out of the mountains to attend. The large Communist army would arrive in a few days, they said, and offered to hide the priests in the mountains. The Fathers declined and gave their extra supplies and clothes to the fleeing Catholics. They also sent the parish records, vestments, and all chalices except one (for Mass) into the Catholic villages of Koo Pen and Shaan Cha, about twelve miles away in the mountains.

The last wedding was on January 8, with the newly married couple joining the race for the mountains. The big battle would be fought within twenty-four hours. A few guerrillas dug in behind the mission to wait for the 3,000 Communists bringing mortar, hand grenades and machine guns. The battle lasted eighty minutes, and the Maryknollers figured the guerrillas had lost when they saw the Communists running over the hill and past the mission, screaming and yelling. One group beat on the mission door.

"Who's there?" Father Edmonds asked and opened the door to face approximately 400 young Communist soldiers. All were well trained, mannerly. They also spoke Mandarin dialect and asked dozens of questions by writing in Chinese. Each soldier carried a fountain pen. They asked such questions as, "Where are you from?" "Are there many poor people in the United States?" "Don't worry. In six months, we are going to liberate your country—the good people—from the bad government and bad army, and everything will be good."

During their three weeks in the mission the Communists

decorated the building with propaganda pictures of women marching on Washington, D.C., with brooms and sticks. Another poster showed President Truman standing on a box, grinning and dropping atomic bombs.

The Communist leader was a short, bloated man of forty-five whom the priests named "General Cheung." He was mannerly but confiscated the priests' cameras.

"After all," he insisted, "they could be used to spy." He asked how to use a camera, and thanked the priests repeatedly. Then he pranced around, snapping the shutter at everything that moved.

The dirt streets were filled with despair as relatives of defeated soldiers staggered back to their homes for slavery, but some soon committed suicide with poisonous berries. Many church members and guerrillas were led into the mission with their hands and necks tied. The chapel became the death cell.

Father Edmonds was helpless. At 2 P.M. one Sunday everyone—priests, children, and prisoners—were taken outside for a "trial." Thirteen men the priests knew to be kind were put on a platform.

A Communist asked, "People, what shall we do with these criminals? These bandits!"

Following the Communist system of mixing cadres in crowds, several of the ringers yelled, "Kill them! kill them!"

"Then it is the people's will," the "judge" announced. "The will of the new country of the people! These criminals must die!"

The condemned were placed on their knees in a kind of

football huddle. Every known relative was circled around them. A Communist soldier stood over each kneeling prisoner and fired at him repeatedly until his face was completely mutilated.

"I cannot . . . I really cannot begin to explain the looks of those horrified, paralyzed people," Father Edmonds confessed.

Two days later approximately 2,000 simple, law-abiding human beings were executed and many of the bodies quartered; others met slower deaths by being sent to a prison filled with people dying of smallpox. The commandant played a violin and sang himself to sleep after the daily ordeal.

The mission, which was used as the "courthouse," soon became an ammunition dump and overflowed with troops. As new soldiers arrived, the priests were subjected to threats, screams, and questioning, although they were never physically mistreated. Sixteen-year-old soldiers would kick the door and scream, but as they searched the priests they would whisper, "I'm sorry to have to do this. They're watching me."

One night the commandant stopped his music and sent for the Maryknoll priests. He was, he said, a man of his word and very happy to reimburse the Fathers for their cameras. He showed them all the religious articles the priests had sent to the mountains.

"See," he snapped, "stolen by guerrilla bandits. We recover for you. Bring back."

General Cheung examined the articles, but discarded a record book of church members' names that the Communists' intelligence would have treasured. (Father Edmonds later buried it.) He also had additional glad tidings, he said, as he placed a hand on Father Edmonds' shoulder. "You very good camera teacher," he said, "and I thank you for learn picture-taking. Now, how you like to go back to America?"

The general was a man of his word and wrote a letter of introduction to the government at Pengnam, requesting that the priests be given special consideration for exit permits. The priests packed and left To Pong the morning of March 17. But their hopes were short-lived. Communist guards stopped them for identity papers near Sz Wong and demanded, "Who gave you permission to leave To Pong?"

The priests offered General Cheung's letter. The local cadre called in another general, who maintained belligerently that they were "government property" and ordered them back to To Pong. When Fathers Edmonds and Karlovecius returned to their mission, they found that their general "friend" had been replaced. The priests and their belongings were immediately locked in the attic.

The soldiers had little to occupy their time and remodeled the rooms by papering them with pages from the priests' books and magazines. "You would find a page of Noldin's moral theology plastered next to a page of *Look*," Father Edmonds recalls, "or a page out of *Time* next to the Bible."

Outside the tiny single-paned window they could see other troops drilling and being lectured.

"America is preparing to invade China," one soldier preached, "they're already in Korea. Truman, Wall Street, the U.S. Paper Tiger and all the running dogs of America must be liquidated."

Another soldier replaced him and screamed that he had just returned from Korea, and that almost every little girl there had been raped by the Americans, and that many of the priests had raped little girls in the mountains not too far from To Pong.

"Those running dogs in the attic there have done the same thing. That's why we can't allow them freedom to roam around and preach. They called this a mission, those running-dog priests in there. This was a house of prostitution."

Then another Communist showed the non-Catholics the techniques of the confessional. "You just can't imagine the obscenities that took place between the priests and Catholics in those dark rooms," he said. "And besides that, they gave the women a drug they called medicine to prevent them from bearing children—another U.S. plot to weaken our New China."

After six weeks of small daily portions of rice and greens, Fathers Edmonds and Karlovecius were allowed in the mission yard. Then an officer said perhaps they would like to visit the opening of the new Tsz Tong School down the hill.

Father Edmonds sat on a school bench in the rear. The children sang, "All Hail to Mao and the New China." The second song was, "Down With Americans—Liquidate the Capitalists." They formed their newly introduced snake dance by lining up behind each other with their bodies leaning forward and their arms swinging, taking two steps forward, then one back, to the rhythm of drums. Then they sat down and pounded their desks. "Down with the Catholic Church, down with the priests and their God!" Four of the little girls had been in Father Edmonds' school the year before.

Finally the priests were informed that they would be permitted to leave after they had been investigated thoroughly. The investigation consisted of Red soldiers coming into the attic and spitting at them; former mission employees were brought in to relate tales of "spying, stealing and brutality."

Next day Father Edmonds was told to walk down a certain street for exercise. He was ambushed with rocks by the Communist teacher and students, who sang "Smash the Foreign Devils." When the priest returned to the attic, he heard a call from the courtyard. He looked out the window, and the children broke it with rocks.

Meanwhile Father Karlovecius became ill, and Father Edmonds got permission to take him to a government doctor. The doctor said the illness was imaginary. Father Edmonds argued that it was not. The doctor—in a typical *volte-face*—said the priest was completely correct and that he had been wrong. "Now be sure," the doctor said suavely, "to go home [the attic] and get plenty of fresh air and sunshine. And try to eat at least four or five well-balanced meals—many different foods—every day."

Father Edmonds received another report saying he could leave, but he had been told this now for five months. Finally the departure was confirmed for the second week of October, and he was allowed to see his parishioners for the last time. When he returned to his attic cell, a young boy was waiting for him.

The boy insisted that he wanted to be baptized. "Yes," he said, "I know what happened." His cousin, a Catholic, had been pulled out of the seminary and into the Communist army; two of his friends were serving life sentences for considering the priesthood; his uncle had been executed, his father jailed.

After convincing Father Edmonds that he was willing to suffer the consequences, the boy insisted he had studied for two years and remembered his catechism. Although Father Edmonds met with him secretly, he delayed the ritual until the boy slipped back one night and said the soldiers had left. On October 11, in the complete darkness of his attic, Father Edmonds performed the ceremony.

But as usual the priests' departure date passed. The only difference on this day was the scene under their window. Several women were placed in baskets and rolled to death; bamboo spikes were driven under the fingernails of others to force them to "confess."

The torture session ended shortly before Thanksgiving. The two priests had a Thanksgiving dinner of greens, but were surprised at midnight by three local Chinese, smuggling them a basket filled with stuffed duck, bread, fudge and jam.

The next morning Father Karlovecius received his orders to go to Pengnam. There he met other priests who were being expelled. Each was put through a long, trying experience. All of their possessions were taken "for the next native church," the officer said. The Communist barked, "What are you foreign devils trying to do—steal items that belonged to the church?" Then the guards circulated the rumor that the group had murdered nineteen babies "for fun" near Canton. There was little sleeping that night; a crowd milled outside, making such remarks as, "Let's drag those foreign devils out for trial," or "No, let's feed them—feed them bullets."

Father Edmonds, meanwhile, remained alone in the attic, and additional guards were put on his door on Christmas Eve. The priest asked to go outside for Christmas, and the cadre obliged. "I've selected a perfect place for you to visit." He grinned. "The pigpen." Ironically, twenty Catholics who were hiding nearby attended the Father's Mass and left before the guard made him return to the attic.

On January 2, 1951, Father Edmonds was led out and inspected for weapons. "Tell us where your machine gun is." "Where's your spy equipment?" "Where's your list of spies?"

He was finally told that he, too, was being sent to Pengnam. Although his leg muscles were weak from the year's close confinement, he was forced to walk the entire thirty-five miles.

By the time he reached the Pengnam police station, Father Edmonds was near collapse, but the agenda called for solid hours of incessant questioning and followed the Communist pattern: "Look, we know you hid your guns. Where are they? Where did you bury your gold bars?"

When the guards finally tired, they locked up Father Edmonds with other missionaries. Next morning all of the priests were put on a boat for Canton, where the questioning ordeal was repeated in detail. At last they boarded the slow Canton-Hong Kong train for the interminable ninety-mile trip to the bridge at Lowu.

Father Edmonds was taken off the train at the Communist border station. He could see the Hong Kong side. Freedom! He showed his travel documents, signed by the Communists, but his captors inflicted one final touch of agony. The "imperialist" could see freedom, but he could not have it immediately. Two long, tortuous hours later a guard motioned for the ragged priest to get across the Hong Kong border.

# 3.

## BACK IN BUSINESS

HONG KONG was only a terminal for Mary-
knoll missionaries during the great exodus from Communist
China. The British colony was overcrowded with unemployed pastors, and the priests had no alternative but to
leave. The sick were returned to Maryknoll for recuper-
ation. The able-bodied briefly rested in the three-story
brick Maryknoll House located atop a hill on Hong Kong
Island, directly across from the Stanley Prison and over-
looking an ancient little fishing village and six insignificant
Communist-held islands.

When Father Edmonds arrived at the Stanley House,
he found that the priests awaiting reassignment to South
America and the free countries of Asia had all known experiences similar to his and were willing to discuss them.

One was Father Howard D. Trube, a square-jawed, crew-cut man born on New York's East 15th Street in 1914. He had lost fifty pounds while being imprisoned in a pigpen for three months.

Father Trube had been assigned to the Philippines, but a resident visa to the islands required two months to be processed, and his vacation in Hong Kong became longer than he had planned. He was not inactive, however—not all of his Chinese parishioners had remained under the Communists. Several families had escaped en masse and gathered on the same squatter hillside in Hong Kong. Two of the refugees were his native catechists, and one of them telephoned the Maryknoll house.

"You know I'll be right over there," Father Trube told him. "Now let's see . . . that's right . . . you can't very well give directions to an unnamed hillside, can you? Look, how about meeting me on the Kowloon side of the Star ferry?"

Father Trube walked briskly down the steep, winding concrete road leading to the bus line, transferred to the Kowloon ferry, and an hour later was reunited with the two catechists and five or six refugees from his Ng Fa mission. But To Wan Leng (his Chinese name, meaning "To Save Souls") was depressed as he toured the squatter area. He passed a math teacher begging for cooliework and saw another acquaintance being chased for stealing a dried fish.

"But, *Shen Foo* [Father]," the catechist said, "we look for work. Coolie, anything, all day, but nobody hire.

Children can't starve. We must get food. Begging is no good. There is nothing to beg for."

Not only were refugees living in flimsy cardboard and tar-paper shacks, but many had also been wiped out by a fire that had completely leveled one hillside. The government responded to the disaster by giving the burned-out squatters cards entitling them to buy or rent space in resettl ent areas built by government and private contractors. The cards were as useless as Communist money in Hong Kong. Most refugees didn't have enough money for a meal, let alone a down payment on a house.

That night Father Trube explained the refugees' plight to Father Thomas Malone, Maryknoll Superior in Hong Kong. "Look, nobody's taking care of these people," Father Trube said. "They need both material and spiritual help."

Father Malone, along with Maryknoll's superior-general in the United States, had already made applications to begin parishes in Hong Kong. At this time Archbishop Riberi, Papal Internuncio to China, was expelled from Nanking to Hong Kong, and Father Malone recommended that he inspect the squatter camp. The prelate was equally disturbed and informed the Most Reverend Lawrence Bianchi, Bishop of Hong Kong.

Bishop Bianchi welcomed Maryknoll's offer to assist in refugee areas, but emphasized that "it should be somebody who knows and understands the people."

"Father Trube has been out there several times," Father Malone said, "seeing some of his old friends."

"Then why don't you keep Father Trube here instead of sending him to the Philippines?" the bishop asked.

Bishop Bianchi was familiar with Father Trube's work. Ten years earlier, when Father Bianchi had been vicar-general of the order's territory in Free China and imprisoned with his Italian colleagues during World War II, Father Trube had arranged for his release and then led him on a five-day walk to a safe zone 120 miles away. After the war Bishop Bianchi feared there might be local reaction against his returning to China. The Maryknoll priest solved that too. Since Father Trube was the first American in the liberated China area, he automatically received friendly receptions. He installed Father Bianchi in the place of honor, thereby removing any doubts or local reactions.

Father Bianchi, now the bishop, agreed to Maryknoll beginning parishes in Hong Kong, provided it made its own arrangements for land.

The Maryknoll purpose, like that of all mission groups, is to gain converts for its church, but the priests saw that these refugees needed material help before anything. And it required more than gall to solicit charity for refugees; Hong Kong itself needed a handout. Although Britain had recognized the Communist regime, it had scrupulously enforced the United Nations' embargo on the export of strategic materials to the mainland when the Chinese invaded Korea. So as trade dwindled in 1950–1951, refugees increased. Some businesses panicked into filing petitions of bankruptcy; others transferred operations to Tokyo, Singapore or Manila. Many people were writing off Hong Kong as insolvent—sufficient grounds for tabling the refugee problem until better days.

Nevertheless Maryknoll applied Thomas Merton's dictum: "It is easy enough to tell the poor to accept poverty as God's will. But if you want them to believe it, try to share some of their poverty. And see if you can accept it as God's will yourself." 1215983

The mission rented a 10-by-15-foot room perched on a hillside in Kowloon's Tung Tau Tsuen area, and on March 16, 1952, Father Trube became the first American known to live in a Chinese squatter camp.

The priest cleaned and whitewashed the $17-a-month[1] room the best he could. During the day the shack was a community center, chapel, dispensary, reading room and headquarters where refugee needs might be processed. At night, when he unfolded a roll-away bed, it was his sleeping quarters.

After another fire leveled a nearby section, Dan Wakefield, Government Resettlement Director, issued victims white cards verifying the fact that they were squatters and eligible for possible resettlement. Father Trube also was classified a squatter and given a card. "But I don't want to resettle," the priest said. "I want to expand right here."

The initial expansion came when Cardinal Spellman gave Maryknoll $1,250, half of a fee he had received from *Collier's* magazine for writing an article on refugees. It was spent for three connecting huts. By August the unsightly

---

[1] Unless otherwise noted, all figures will be in United States currency. One Hong Kong dollar is worth 17½ U. S. cents.

35

four shacks became the first Bishop Ford Memorial Center, named in honor of Maryknoll's Bishop Francis X. Ford, who died in a Canton prison a few weeks before the dedication ceremony.[2] The four small rooms had removable partitions and served as library, clinic, parish employment office, weaving and furniture schools.

The government, realizing the value of Maryknoll's contribution, donated land for a permanent Maryknoll center. The catch was that it was 160 feet above sea level and classified as an obstruction to airplanes. The height limit for buildings in the area was 150 feet. So work gangs, paid out of American donations, carved 45 feet off the hill. Donations to Maryknoll were insufficient to complete the project, but the Hong Kong government volunteered to give the mission half the building cost and to lend Maryknoll 30 percent of this interest free.

Thus, less than a year after Father Trube had joined the refugees, he had a six-room concrete school[3] that converted into a church on Sundays.

It was the first modern Maryknoll building among refugees in Hong Kong, and was designed to expand into the mission's largest parish. The surroundings, though, didn't exactly lend inspiration. The view from Father Trube's kitchen-office was a Chinese cemetery carved out of a hillside, and by custom open to wind and water—a little too open. One of the landslides there buried twenty-one people alive. To the east was a granite quarry which furnished

[2] Father Trube served under Bishop Ford in China.
[3] The four shacks that served as the original Bishop Ford Center later were fenced and given to lepers.

building material; to the north was jagged Limerock Mountain; to the south—the foot of Tung Tau Tsuen—was the infamous Kowloon Walled City.

Walled City was a dark, two-acre ghetto containing 5,000 people. Most paths—actually the word "streets" would have been an exaggeration—were so narrow that pedestrians turned sideways when they met. The lowest parts were open sewers. Every vice known to man—and a few that weren't known to most—was practiced there.

Five- and six-year-old children played cards and gambled on the Walled City paths. Opium or heroin were as accessible as newspapers. Injections were given in doorways. Brothels displayed merchandise cafeteria style. In some narrow spots young girls were pulled into doorways and men were robbed. Babies were sold. Kidnapping and blackmailing were arranged by fee by remnants of the old Shanghai Green Gang. New forbidden secret societies—namely the Fourteen K [4] gang—sprang up. These societies, which bind members with blood oaths and sometimes demand murder to prove allegiance, became so ruthless that bodies were regularly found in public latrines.

Neither the Hong Kong police nor Father Trube could do much. It was a no man's land; the police could not enter legally. When the Kowloon and New Territories portions of Hong Kong were leased from China in 1898, the old Walled City had been excluded, being left in the

[4] Police reports indicate the Fourteen K gang was formed by refugees from the mainland in 1949 and had 80,000 members, second largest in the colony. The gang was a reorganization of the Hung Fat Shan Chung Yee Tong, which was started by General Kot Siu Wong in Kwangtung province.

37

control of a mandarin. As years passed, the mandarin died and the office was not filled by the Imperial government, which fell to the Nationalists, and they in turn bowed to the Communists.[5] Now the secret societies ran the place.

A. V. Gorden, the Hong Kong police officer in charge of that area, told Father Trube that the extent of his legal authority was deporting the worst criminal elements and occasionally trying to maintain some semblance of cleanliness to prevent an epidemic.

With complete control of the Walled City, the gangs next attempted to seize control of the public water taps, located across the street from the Walled City entrance, and charge refugees for their own water. Father Trube had the police chase the gangs back inside the wall. He also helped refugees when the gangs tried to enlist them as morphine and heroin peddlers.

Still, many residents needed help,[6] such as the refugees, and Father Trube included refugees inside the wall when a truckload of food donations arrived. The needy were given cards qualifying them to enter the food line. Father Trube hired a student to distribute the cards until the youngster was attacked by eleven members of the Fourteen K gang. Luckily the boy broke away, barricaded himself in the third floor of a building, and recognized a passing girl as belonging to the Maryknoll church.

"Get the priest," he yelled.

Father Trube ran all the way down the hill and en-

[5] The Supreme Court finally ruled it British territory in 1957.
[6] Sixteen hundred of the Walled City's 5,000 residents were regulars at Maryknoll church by 1962.

countered the leader of the Fourteen K gang, whom he had met before. "Look," the priest said, slowly and deliberately. "You're molesting my worker and you aren't going to get away with it. He works and represents me. If you're poor, you'll get a card. If you aren't, you don't get a thing. I know your names. It won't take five minutes to get the police waiting outside. Unless you want to spend the rest of your lives hiding in this place, then I don't want any more of this."

The gang sulked, cursed, and walked away. They weren't finished, they sneered. But the Fourteen K didn't know they were fighting a priest accustomed to battling hoodlums. Banditry was such a recognized occupation in China that most Maryknoll priests had to learn to outconnive thieves. Particularly Father Trube.

Once four Chinese bandits with drawn guns slipped from behind a building and held up Father Trube and a young boy on a bicycle. The priest decided to bluff them and bellowed, "Don't you dare point those things at me!"

"Keep quiet," they whispered. "You'll alarm the whole neighborhood."

"You hear me now," the priest yelled, "and you'd better not touch that boy on the bike or there'll be real trouble."

"Ah," said the bandit leader, "just a priest. Let's go."

The bandits had terrorized people so easily for years, Father Trube explained, that his sudden yelling had shocked them into leaving. "I guess they'd never heard anything like it," recalled the priest.

Another time a friend intercepted Father Trube and informed him that about twenty bandits were waiting in a teahouse at the bottom of a steep hill. The priest had to continue his trip, so he came down the hill pedaling instead of coasting and was past the teahouse and zigzagging out of gun range before the surprised bandits could shoot.

Father Trube's third escape from bandits was purely providential. The priest had completed a trip to Maryknoll's Ng Fa station and was making the two-day return hike to Shai Chai with his house boy. The boy was carrying the equipment and walking several yards in front of Father Trube. Suddenly there was a yell from behind. A messenger informed the priest that Bishop Ford had arrived at Ng Fa and wanted to see him. He returned to the mission headquarters while the boy continued on to Shai Chai. Father Trube started back the next day and met a search party looking for him. They told him that the bandits had allowed the boy to pass unharmed, thinking the priest was close behind.

The Fourteen K gang's final attack on a Maryknoll parishioner came one Wednesday afternoon when Father Trube was leaving his primary school. He heard screams from his driveway and saw the gang working over a squatter, with short knives. By the time the priest could get to the man's aid, the gang ran. Father Trube got a look at them, but first had to attend to the badly bleeding refugee. The doctor counted eighty-five knife wounds on the man, who had refused to sell dope.

Father Trube, familiar with all kinds of people, imported

a middleman who knew the gang leaders' whereabouts, and gave him a typed list of their names.

"The priest," Father Trube's informant told the gang, "has many copies of this list. Many different places. He wants to have police handcuff you when you come out of Walled City and take you back over China border."

None of the Fourteen K or any of the gangs wanted any part of Red China. The priest had outsmarted Asia's toughest gang.

# 4.

## BRANCHING OUT

**T**HREE months after Father Trube moved into the squatter camp, Maryknoll began its second mission in Hong Kong and named Father Edmonds pastor. The site, called "The End of the Line," was well named. The long-secluded rural area originally was Hing Wa Village in the Chai Wan (Firewood Bay) section. The tract resembled a bottomless bowl—its lower portion was a dock for small sampans and junks.

The extremely steep hillsides had seemed crowded when they held 3,000 people, but Chai Wan's population swelled to 18,000 and was still growing. In addition to being poor, most of the recent refugees in Father Edmonds' area were illiterate and unskilled. When refugees streamed into Hong Kong, they initially sought relatives, then hillsides on Kowloon (mainland side). If unsuccessful at both attempts, they crossed to Hong Kong Island and either remained in the streets or kept wandering. Many refugees settled in the Shaukiwan squatter camp, but Shaukiwan was soon demolished for an industrial site. Chai Wan, entrance to Lyeman Pass or Hong Kong Harbor, was thus the last stop.

When Father Malone requested government land for prospective Maryknoll parishes, he was advised that Chai Wan eventually would be developed. The government filled in some land [the swamp], installed a public water faucet, and gave Maryknoll a deserted army barracks about 13 feet wide and 150 feet long. Father Edmonds, or Man Hin Wing (Shooting Forth Glory), as the Chinese called him, moved into the barracks' west end on March 6, 1952, and converted the remaining portion into a chapel, community center and school.

Unlike Father Trube's area, Father Edmonds did not have any former parishioners to introduce new refugees. No one, to Father Edmonds' knowledge, is known to have escaped from the To Pong area.

There were, however, forty-two persons in the area who said they were Catholic, thereby forming the core of a church. The remainder was mostly pagan, with some Buddhist and Taoist. They huddled outside the window to watch the curious church ceremony, and when Church members came out, they pulled them aside and asked: "What's a Catholic, anyway?" "What's going on?" "Why does this foreigner live with us and run a school?" "Maybe he's up to something."

43

Father Edmonds had little material help to offer refugees. When he received sizable donations of secondhand clothing or medicine, he gave to the neediest. Ironically, his first shipment of American clothing was mostly women's spike-heeled shoes, fancy lingerie and evening gowns that a society organization had given with good intentions. Later some of the refugees were found trying to peddle a beribboned, lacy nightgown in the streets.

As Father Edmonds continued to give without enclosing political propaganda material, the refugees grew less suspicious. The barracks became such a village headquarters that he baptized sixty-nine pagans before the year ended. Those who didn't join the church—called the Star of the Sea parish—still came to Father Edmonds for assistance. The government had published notices that the adjacent public graveyard would be cleared for a future housing settlement. Most people responded by digging up the bones and carrying them away in urns. Some bodies were not reclaimed, and bulldozers piled bones and rocks together. It was a rare night when Father Edmonds didn't answer knocks at his door seven or eight times. The callers insisted ghosts were leaving the graves and planning to carry off people. Sometimes he had to walk through the graveyard alone to convince the refugees there was nothing to fear.

Although there was a small police station in Chai Wan, Father Edmonds made many trips to the downtown jail. Refugees who had managed to scrape up 50 to 75 cents were getting up at 4 A.M., walking a mile to the bus, buying vegetables and reselling them. They couldn't afford both the hawker's license and the vegetables, so the license came second. Sometimes the priest got the people off with a $1 fine, which he had to pay himself; sometimes they were released without a fine.

There were also many requests from parents to "write a letter of introduction for my son to reform school." The children were basically good, but strayed into petty trouble and inevitably grew rowdy when they had to raise themselves while their parents searched for food. Father Edmonds was able to keep several boys' names off the police blotters and thus make their future lives a little more bearable. And many of his trips to police stations ceased when he organized his Dominic Savio Club for boys.

Back in Kowloon, across Limerock Mountain from Bishop Ford Center, the third Maryknoll parish began in December of 1952. It was on an even taller peak called Ngau Tau Kok, which some cab drivers claimed would nearly strip gears. Father John Curran started the parish, was followed by Fathers Carroll Quinn and John McGinn, until late March 1954, when Father Arthur Dempsey became the permanent tenant. A six-foot, 225-pound, white-haired man born March 22, 1903, in New York's Hell's Kitchen (now the entrance to the Lincoln Tunnel), Father Dempsey's biggest contribution in Hong Kong was teaching new employment skills. His initial task, however, required fighting Hong Kong's undesirables.

He was well trained for this. Maryknoll's early missioners

found China more a battlefield than a mission field, and periodically were caught in crossfires.

A typical instance came when raiders attacked the mandarin's troops across from a Maryknoll mission and two Fathers arranged a truce. But the local mandarin ignored the agreement and fired at the intruders while the priests held a white flag. The enraged invaders reassaulted, and Maryknoll's compound became the mandarin's sanctuary. A Father slapped the mandarin, hid him in the rice bin, then brazenly talked the attacking general into leaving.

Thus Hong Kong's professional thieves were soft touches for the veteran Dempsey. Since Father Dempsey's parish was situated in a new area on the outskirts of the city, he became a favorite target for professional tramps and their manufactured, amazingly pitiful stories.

He got his first case one night when he heard a little boy yell, "Hit Shen Foo! Hit Shen Foo!"

Father Dempsey hurried outside where a robust young man was shaking a smaller priest by the collar. His story had been recognized as phony and he had been refused a handout.

"There was only one thing to do," Father Dempsey recalled. "I grabbed the punk by the collar and the seat of his pants, shook him till I was certain his teeth rattled, and then bounced him down the steps. Then I went to the bottom of the steps to meet him and asked if he wanted a little more.

"Funny thing." Father Dempsey laughed. "The fakers are the only ones with any really wild stories such as you'd expect in movies. They make themselves too obvious. And they invariably pull their acts here at night when there usually aren't any police around."

One of these performances came on a March evening when Father Dempsey had stepped outside for some air before beginning his correspondence. A skilled actor was poised by the church gate. When he saw the priest come out, he began sprinting toward him, hollering, "Communist China! Communist China! Where are they?"

"Where are what, young man?" Father Dempsey replied.

"Communist guards," the boy said, led Father Dempsey over to the railing, pointed beyond a church, and explained how he had just climbed the Communist border fence. The guards had been chasing him and had nearly shot him four times (it's thirty-three miles from the border).

"Now, thank God," the boy said, "I've reached safety."

"Yes, and that's wonderful," Father Dempsey said, shaking his hand. "And now you're perfectly safe and free from the Communists. Nothing to worry about."

"But, Father," the boy pleaded, again pointing, "I have some friends I can go to down there. But I need money to get there."

"Why, son," Father Dempsey said softly, "it's just a short walk. But look, I'll get the car and drive you down."

The boy became so incensed that he called the priest a colorful string of blasphemous names and threatened to fight. Two off-duty policemen still in uniform passed by, and the tramp ran. The police stopped him. He had $500

47

and a Hong Kong identification card showing that he had been in the colony for five years.

Another evening about nine Father Dempsey answered a knock on the door. A thin young man who appeared to be badly wounded stood there. His face, hands and shirt were red with blood.

"I also have bad TB," he gasped. "Please, I beg you, give me ten dollars to go to Queen Mary Hospital."

"Just a second, son," Father Dempsey said. Since there wasn't a doctor at his mission, Father Dempsey phoned Father Trube's parish, which had a doctor on duty Wednesday evenings.

"Just wanted to check with you to see if the doctor is still there," Father Dempsey said. "I'm bringing a young boy over. Bleeding badly."

"If he's about five foot five," Trube replied, "and a hundred pounds, has a white shirt soaked in blood, his left leg all bloody, and his face smeared in blood, you won't get him to come over here."

"How'd you know?" Father Dempsey asked.

"Well," Father Trube answered, "the doctor smelled him a mile away. He buys a couple of pennies' worth of pig's blood and visits a different clinic every night." [1]

Another big, six-foot, 220-pounder, Father Peter A. Rielly, of Roxbury, Massachusetts, moved into a loft in a section

---

[1] Father Bernard Meyer, one of Maryknoll's first group in China, had his personal screening test. He simply roared in colorful Chinese at each man asking for a handout. If the beggar stood his ground, the priest discounted him as a panhandler and provided a meal.

called Kowloonstai (Little Kowloon), to begin Maryknoll's fourth community center. "The biggest problem," explained Father Rielly, "naturally was poverty. They were so poor they were suspicious of the world. I really didn't have anything much in the way of material help to give them at first, and they thought I was up to some trick. Even when I gave out pills or had medicine or helped in any way. They were the most suspicious group I ever encountered. Until I got the break."

The "break" came one September Saturday. Father Rielly was operating the shack as a "clinic." He heard a disturbance outside and saw the Ya family approaching. The mother was screaming, and a crowd followed. The father was carrying John, their nine-year-old son. One man ran to Father Rielly with the news. Young John, he said, had fallen into an old open well and drowned. The Ho man discovered him, got Mr. Ya, and they pulled him out with ropes.

Mr. Ya laid John on the clinic table, crying, "He's dead, he's dead!" Father Rielly felt John's pulse and there was no sign of life. There was no doctor or ambulance around, but the priest figured he should make some kind of effort. He stretched the boy out on the clinic table.

I guess artificial respiration would be the best, Father Rielly said to himself, even if I've never done it before.

As he began his version of artificial respiration, a man pulled on his arms and said, "*Mo yung* [No use]." The crowd increased and everyone chanted "*Mo yung*." Nevertheless, Father Rielly had decided to continue for thirty minutes. A few minutes before the time limit expired, water

49

and foam suddenly spurted out of John's mouth. Ten minutes later the boy started gasping. Five minutes later he was crying, and a half hour later he was home.

The parents, both pagans, later returned to the pastor to settle an argument. Each violently argued that he or she was right, although both believed in *shaang sz meng*, which means life and death are already determined. The mother insisted that John had been saved by the assistance of God. The father shook his fist and said that it was the priest's secular knowledge.

Father Rielly agreed with both. "God must have helped," he said.[2]

The genial pastor's other experiences helped him settle a milder argument with other Maryknollers. Some priests flatly contended that they were in the poorest of poor Hong Kong neighborhoods. Father Rielly not only convinced his colleagues that he was in the poorest area, but he had verification that stealing was its leading occupation.

He once had $1,400 to pay the construction crew for the Maryknoll Fathers School. He pinned the money inside his pants' pocket, folded the pants under his pillow, and of course locked the door and hooked the chain. When he woke the next morning, the pants had been removed.

Father Rielly called the Kowloon police. Four men came and strolled around nonchalantly. Suddenly one of the policemen's eyes began to sparkle. He went up to the deep blue chapel window and grinned. "Ah," he said, "a perfect

[2] The entire Ya family became Catholics, and John graduated from Primary 6 in 1961. The family brings John to Father Rielly for an annual visit.

clue. An excellent fingerprint. We will have to take your pretty window to headquarters to examine the fingerprint. That should help us catch the thief."

"Take the whole building, if it will help," Father Rielly said. "Sure was a break, you getting that fingerprint."

The priest never saw the "cops" or window again.

He did, however, see a newspaper story about a criminal who had been arrested carrying $1,400. The pastor told his story to the police chief. "Can you give us a description, in detail, of the money?" the police chief asked.

Naturally the priest couldn't.

Another case involved a Sister nurse at Father Rielly's clinic who had been saving for a $500 contribution to another clinic. On the day the savings reached $500, somebody broke in and stole them. Father Rielly called the police for the disturbed Sister. The policemen strolled around with a flashlight—it was noon—and promised to investigate every possible lead. They seemed to be working on the case when a policeman telephoned two days later and said he had "good news." Father Rielly immediately put the Sister on the phone.

"Yes, it's excellent news," he explained. "We've arrested an ex-criminal. A very good suspect."

"Oh, you mean I might get my money back," the Sister said excitedly.

"No, no, lady, nothing like that," the policeman said. "We've only found somebody who might be guilty."

He was not guilty and nobody ever called again.

Two months later Father Rielly was spending one of his

rare nights at the Maryknoll headquarters in Stanley and was telling the priests about the thieves. "At least." He laughed in his genial style. "I'll be safe tonight."

After dressing the next morning, he reached for his wallet. It was gone. He later found it, empty, under a brick.

He borrowed bus and ferry money. When he got to his room, it had been ransacked of his food and personal belongings.

When the Maryknoll School was finally ready to open, Father Rielly decided to hire the best night watchman available. Although the building was surrounded by a 6-foot fence, the priest wanted reinforcements. "I want the two most vicious dogs in the history of the colony," he told a Chinese helper. When he saw the dogs' flashing teeth and frightening appearance, he was satisfied. There was never a single robbery. Then one day the dogs were missing. A Walled City gang had baited them, then lassoed them with a wire attached to a pipe. Roast *kau* (dog) is a local Chinese delicacy.[3]

Four established parishes had only a foot in the door, and Maryknoll could see the magnitude of the job ahead. The endless stream of refugees continued to inundate Hong Kong, and for most of them there was still not even a place to sleep.

[3] Hong Kong police today fine anyone guilty of eating, cooking or possessing dog meat $1.75. "Good dog meat," such as young black Chow, brings about 13 cents a pound.

# 5.

## JUST A PLACE TO SLEEP TONIGHT

REFUGEES carried their blankets and sometimes a pot and led their children as they wandered the
streets of Hong Kong, seeking food or work. When shops
closed for the night (and most close late), they huddled
in doorways or under porch eaves. In many areas sidewalk
space was so crowded that people slept in the streets. The
constant exposure was deadly, and refugees were usually
identified by racking coughs.

Their needs were almost too monumental for compre-
hension: food, shelter, medicine, employment, a few dollars, eventual education and the return of self-respect. Most
Chinese consider themselves well off if they can provide
food and bed space for their families. But these uninvited
migrants were so desperate that impoverished people exist-

ing in crowded sampans only slightly larger than canoes pitied them.

Suppose disaster has struck your community. Your bank has collapsed; transportation has ended; you have only a few hours in which to evacuate your wife and six small children. You walk and walk. Eventually you fight your way onto a freight train and arrive with a few personal belongings, but with neither food nor money—in a swollen city filled with commotion and depression. You see no travelers'-aids or relatives or friends—only handpainted signs reading: PLEASE DO NOT ENTER TO SEEK EMPLOYMENT or THERE ARE NO JOBS OF ANY KIND!

This was the refugees' dilemma. Luckier and better-off Chinese found temporary shelter with friends and relatives. Overcrowding was so bad that most tiny homes, or rather rooms, were subdivided into four cubicles by drawing white lines. Shelves were fastened to walls for beds, and even then people slept in shifts. Every place was so packed that it inspired the question, "Say, isn't it pretty crowded in there?"

"Well," the reply went, "wasn't too bad until last week. Then the Wong family over in the corner started taking in roomers."

Most of this million, however, had nowhere to turn. They followed man's most primitive instinct—roadside cover for the night; and these makeshift homes became satellite towns. Additionally, money was not the only gap between needing land and acquiring it. All Hong Kong land is owned by the Crown and merely leased—and there was no land available except for peaks, ravines and hills that resembled upside-down ice-cream cones and were impractical for normal use. Besides the desperate who climbed these and built their lean-tos against rocks and trees or dug caves, others wandered into places around the Walled City where Father Trube's parish shack stood, and threw up lean-tos against buildings. Still others provided shelter with chicken crates, discarded tin, and sacks slung over frames. Refugees who occasionally found a day's cooliework built some of the better-class shacks—of tar paper.

A chimney was a rare luxury, and the resulting uncontrollable fires were almost as constant as daylight and dark. During the first four years of the refugee influx there were 141 fires classified as major, and 142,000 people who managed huts, shops or cubbyhole businesses were homeless again. On Christmas night 1953, a 45-acre refugee camp burned like a seared pine tree. Fifty-eight thousand refugees were back in the streets by morning.

Fireproof homes were the only solution. The Hong Kong government agreed heartily, but questioned the justification of mass housing of refugees when, after all, it was short of public funds to help its own citizens. And it was against policy to enter into housing programs. Moreover, a housing project would exceed the cost of new projects: an airport that was virtually an obligation ($110 million), a water reservoir ($125 million), a hospital ($50 million) and reclaimed land from the sea ($30 million).

Although uncommitted to definite resettlement programs, the government welcomed volunteer work. It received its first proposal from the Maryknoll Sisters, who worked with the Maryknoll Fathers. The Sisters had been in Hong Kong since 1920, operating schools and convents. But now there were additional Sisters, themselves refugees from China, and they decided to venture into the social-service field begun by the Fathers.

Sister Imelda held a critique on where to begin, and the conclusion was that the first permanent contribution should be housing. Sister Imelda's written request to the Land Authority was pleasantly implemented; the government gave the Sisters one-fifth of an acre of hillside in the unsettled—and somewhat unexplored—area of King's Park, Homantin, to be used for resettlement cottages. Thus the Sisters became the first volunteer agency in Hong Kong to undertake a housing venture for refugees.

With the spirit of perpetual Fuller Brush salesmen, the Sisters solicited contributions and began building little houses out of sand brick. The initial cottage, adjacent to a newly installed public water faucet, went to the Lee family. The husband had been a major in the Nationalist army, had taught military strategy, and written military articles for Chinese magazines. His profession was not an asset in Hong Kong. It was, if anything, a hindrance.

Certainly there was no demand for military personnel. Many businesses looked on putting former Chinese Nationalist officers on the payroll, even if they were qualified, as an unnecessary risk with the Communists so precariously close.

The head of the Lee family was hawking preserved fish when the Sisters gave him the first house, loaned him enough money for a driver's license, and uncovered a lead for a chauffeur's job. He got it. But just as the Lees recovered their dignity, the husband's cough became so bad that he lost his job. The doctor said Lee had slept in the streets too long and had tuberculosis. Then the Sisters loaned Mrs. Lee money for a foot-pedaled sewing machine. She not only repaid the loan in full, but earned her family's living by making pajamas that the Sisters marketed. And even though the father could not work, he would not allow himself to be supported by his wife. He took the Maryknoll pincushion-making course and made more pincushions at home than anyone in the village.

The Sisters were not only building homes in King's Park, but also added 18 houses in Father Trube's Tung Tau Tsuen area. But by the time they had completed 71 cottages at a cost of $400 each, it was evident the program would die for simple lack of money. Moreover, Father Trube emphasized the fact that they needed a "permanent crash program." Even if Maryknoll tripled its housing production—which was impossible without additional funds—most people still would have to remain in the shacks.

They weren't in them long. A typhoon eliminated 2,400 more shacks one morning before breakfast.

Maryknoll's do-it-yourself emergency housing program began. Father Trube showed the squatters and the daily refugee arrivals how to build simple homes. The basic requirement was a little lumber—usually six or eight 12-by-12 boards—for a frame which was covered with tin sheets. The complete price of the prefabricated home was under $25.

"Usually when a family lost everything in a fire or typhoon, or escaped from the Communists," Father Trube said, "we tried to mold them back into a family again. This much—twenty-five dollars—wasn't too expensive, and it gave them a completely new start. We generally added a set of clothing, maybe a pot, a couple of bed boards and a sack of rice. Eventually we must have put up twenty-five thousand houses like that."

Nevertheless, Maryknoll also wanted its Hong Kong work to be as permanent as possible, even though the colony's New Territories lease will expire in 1997. It wanted durable homes that were absolutely fireproof—and much cheaper than the $400 mansions.

Father Trube tried an experiment. There was a granite quarry only 150 yards from his parish. He learned that Kowloon granite solidifies when exposed to air and that bulldozers could mine it in its original state. He had the material and plenty of unemployed laborers. The first house was to be a community demonstration. If he received donations and government approval, lifetime homes could be built cheaply.

The trial model house was put up for a Cantonese-speaking man named Cheung Sum Bak, whose family of six lived in the streets while he sought day-to-day cooliework. Most days he didn't find any. Father Trube invited other prospective home owners from his parish as helpers. They planned a 14-by-17-foot structure and built it with granite, cement and a mud-lime plaster in nine and a half days. The wife was so excited that she slipped the family's shopping bag of belongings into the home while the men were still plastering. The three-year-old son nearly encased himself by stumbling into a plaster bucket.

The refugee wasn't the only one excited. Father Trube totaled the exact cost—$122. This, he said, is the solution.

The home put the Cheung family back on its feet. The husband eventually landed a teaching job in a private school, divided the building into three partitioned "rooms," whitewashed it, and continued a steady improvement program until 1957, when he moved into a better home and relinquished his house to a new refugee.

Maryknoll's low-cost housing plan was an immediate success, and similar cottages rose as fast as donations arrived. It encouraged people to help. A pagan family which had escaped from China donated enough for 10 houses in the memory of its late father; a Belgian group mailed money for 12 houses. The Hong Kong Actors' Guild staged a benefit performance which enabled Maryknoll to build 20 cottages. Everybody—from British Air Force officers to basement-laundry operators—contributed. The Hong Kong government was so impressed that it contracted for 500 Maryknoll-type houses and gave them to refugees at low rentals.

Then a problem arose. The chairman of the Hong Kong Urban Council, K. M. A. Barnett, and others announced that many squatters were neither destitute nor refugees. Barnett charged that some Hong Kong residents were selling their living quarters to refugees, using the money to start their own businesses, and then moving into refugee resettlement tracts. Barnett won few supporters, particularly among the Maryknoll Fathers and Sisters. They knew people with money would not live in such filth or eat discarded chicken feet and fish heads. A few local Chinese did sell their homes to refugees who had foreseen the Communist victory early enough to deposit money in Hong Kong banks. The sellers experienced problems finding new homes, but only a tiny fraction moved into squatter areas.

Then a larger problem arose. After Maryknoll had built eighty-five cottages in the Tung Tau Tsuen area, the Hong Kong government concluded that the land was too precious for one-story cottages and passed a resolution against additional cottage construction.[1] A well-founded slogan, "Save the land," was circulated.

The government pointed out that cottages would occupy the same space as a large apartment house, but also contended that building space was nonexistent.

Land soon was cleared. After a fire in 1954 drove 53,000 refugees back to the streets—followed by another fire that destroyed 24,000 huts—the Hong Kong Housing Authority was created and began to function as a commercial enterprise. The government allocated land at one third its market value to volunteer housing projects and supplemented it with low-interest loans.

Then "Seven-Storey Mountains"—as the new housing quarters were named—replaced rock mountains. Hong Kong virtually came to a standstill at noon and at 5 P.M.—called "blast time"—as rocky hillsides came down and the sea was

---

[1] Thereafter Maryknoll's new houses, which now were being constructed under the auspices of Catholic Relief Services, were restricted to rural areas or replacements for homes destroyed by typhoons or fire.

filled in to create land. The government began seven-story housing projects, each shaped exactly like an H. It charged nominal rents designed to recover the building cost in forty years, or $2.83 for an "average apartment room" and up to $7.09 for what refugees considered a "penthouse." Maryknollers and other volunteers were assigned the rooftops and lower-floor partitions for schools, nurseries and clinics.

By 1962, the government had built over 200 blocks housing 469,000 refugees, or over one-seventh of the entire population. But even these figures are deceptive. Children are counted as "half a person," and relatives smuggle in so many new arrivals from China that the buildings sound like giant beehives. And the government is building and opening a new block, each providing a minimum space for 2,200 persons, every ten days.

Maryknoll does not contribute to these resettlement "mountains" today, but if it had not built its original cottages, many of those who live in them might not be around.

Housing was one of Hong Kong's gigantic problems. Employment matched it in size and immediacy.

# 6.

## JUST A CHANCE TO WORK

HONG Kong, whose only natural resource is people, was already seriously plagued by unemployment before the arrival of 1 million refugees with unapplicable skills.

Hunger erases morality, and desperation usually draws a straight line toward stealing. Twenty-four-year-old Wong Kam got a 30-month jail sentence for burglary. Wong asked to say something in court, and the judge granted permission. Wong said, with vehemence, "If I cannot find work when I am released from prison, I will steal again."

When the Hong Kong government's expanding public-works program ultimately began, it was the refugee's largest single employer, but still absorbed only a small fraction of job seekers. It was not a case of Maryknoll, or any volunteer agency, finding jobs for refugees. It was a problem of inventing employment.

Every working level was affected. China, the world's largest country, lost many doctors, lawyers, teachers, dentists, officers, and government officials to Hong Kong. But these people were not allowed to practice their professions in Hong Kong unless they had graduated from Hong Kong University or a British university. Most had not.

Refugee farmers could not farm without land. Those who could afford to own land soon found that Communist China's cut-rate products controlled market prices. Fishermen incurred such competition when a Chinese fleet arrived in Hong Kong that they had to supplement their incomes by selling tropical fish.[1] And no hawker could guarantee himself a daily profit against the competition of teachers, lawyers and soldiers.

"It was a double problem of helping refugees recover their self-respect and giving them a start in something new," observed Father Trube. "Something they could do in Hong Kong. If they could find something to do."

Everything worked against the refugee. Former China businessmen built textile mills, rubber plants and plastic factories in Hong Kong. These new industries furnished overtime employment, but in most cases a man wasn't paid for overtime. Hong Kong has no labor laws, and if one man isn't willing to work 12 to 13 hours a day for $1.25, there are always plenty of men outside waiting for the chance.

Many refugees seeking employment asked Maryknoll priests for a "letter." Since Chinese custom favors applicants

[1] As many as 1 million tropical fish have been flown from Hong Kong annually—mostly to the United States—by "merchandisers."

63

with letters of introduction, they gave refugees more hope. "We used to joke that if we had a Hong Kong dollar for every letter, we could have hired all the refugees ourselves," Father Edmonds recalls.

While many of the letters were more bluff than anything, they frequently did create jobs. Seventeen-year-old Louis Chan supported his widowed mother, two younger sisters and a brother by doing odd jobs and earning 20 cents a night carving ivory. He was drawing on a piece of wrapping paper one day when Father Trube slipped up behind him.

"Say! Not bad," the priest remarked, "not bad at all."

Louis modestly tried to hide the drawing, but Father Trube had another idea. He wrote Louis a letter of introduction as a "very good artist," then checked the classified section of the phone book for places that might need this kind of help. Louis got a job, eventually became a commercial artist, and was able to put his sisters and brother through high school.

The priests found, however, that they must use discretion in giving letters. Father Dempsey discovered that a letter written for a man with a plausible story had been sold for $9.

But job opportunities were still too scarce, even for legitimate letter holders, though mass unemployment did not appear altogether necessary. Cheap labor such as that found in Hong Kong always gave handicraft products a price appeal on the world market. After the United States lifted its embargo in 1952, Hong Kong could market Chinese-type products in the United States if accompanied by a "Certificate of Origin" to verify that they had not been made in Red China.

Many refugees were willing to learn native crafts, but knew they could not sell the products.

Maryknoll went into business. Both the Fathers and Sisters began short training programs in rattan furniture-making, knitting, embroidering and lacquerwork. Home industries quickly sprang up around every parish.

The home-employment innovation made a hit with Maryknoll in America. Father Dempsey, briefly assigned to New York after his twenty-seven years in China, decided to bring his own "factory" when he was transferred to Hong Kong in 1954; he shipped an electrically powered aluminum hand loom to the Ngau Tau Kok parish. The machine, capable of producing 35,000 different high-quality patterns, worked so smoothly that he ordered several more and opened a factory under the charter name of The Pius Company.

Maryknoll paid the students—mostly widows and older unemployed men—80 cents a day while they learned to make tablecloths, stoles and napkins. The class reached 300, which required an outside staff of 12, plus Maryknoll workers such as Brother Gonzaga O'Connor. When students graduated from the six-week course, they had a choice between remaining in the factory at $42 a month, plus the unheard-of benefits of paid overtime, or starting their own businesses at home. A graduate could borrow a hand-operated loom and bale of material and work at home. The pastor gave out such assignments when he received orders from American firms like J. C. Penney, B. Altman & Company, Gertz of Jamaica and Murphy Imports of Detroit.

The firm-speaking Father Dempsey imposed only one restriction—wages could not go for narcotics or gambling. He got an immediate test case.

A husband, or reliable person, must co-sign for a borrowed loom. One husband—a man named Cha'an—thought self-employment was a wonderful way to earn extra money for opium. But when Mrs. Cha'an would not promise her husband the money, he not only refused to sign the contract for the loom but also locked her out and strutted around the neighborhood bragging about it.

When Mr. Cha'an realized that he was making more enemies than supporters, he strolled up the hill to Father Dempsey's office to sign the contract.

"Just give it here," he announced blandly.

"We're not about to let an opium smoker be guarantor on any contract," the husky Father answered firmly. "Either break the habit, or she can't have the loom."

Cha'an walked away.

Three days later Cha'an knocked on Father Dempsey's door and asked, "Is there some place I could go to help me stop smoking?"

The priest sent him to a hospital for the cure, and Mrs. Cha'an became so skilled at making ladies' stoles that later she was hired by a Kowloon factory at double her earnings and eventually moved out of the squatter section.

Meanwhile, the squatter areas became bases for an astonishing variety of new occupations. People of all ages made clothespins and matchboxes of crates; converted raw plastic into combs, soap containers, cigarette cases and flashlight tubes; rolled firecrackers; painted Chinese scrolls, or carved ivory; made wax figures and rattan handbags. It was commonplace to see a small child sitting in a doorway crying, but never stopping his stringing of beads or assembling of plastic flowers.

The advent of these handmade products also necessitated additional shops—anything from cubbyholes in alleys to showrooms in the Far East Mansion Building—and contributed to transforming Hong Kong into a shopper's paradise.

Refugees were promotion minded too. One little man who manufactured plastic eyeglass frames fastened a glossy photograph of Brigitte Bardot on his window and superimposed a pair of frames he had made.

An elderly man who ran an outdoor postcard stand on Nathan Road didn't know English, but decided to utilize a popular tourist promotion gimmick used by the Golden Phoenix Restaurant. He printed, in English, MEMBER OF THE DINERS' CLUB on his box.

Many refugees could not understand English, but copied it meticulously. Father John Cioppa, a new teacher at Bishop Ford Center, wrote a note asking the printer to leave his order of hand-painted Christmas cards and envelopes blank. When he received them, the envelopes bore the engraved return address—NOTHING. The cards were beautifully inscribed NO NAME ON CARD.

Migrants who weren't too destitute quickly opened larger shops in the tourist areas surrounding the Peninsula Hotel. But there was competition in using their own names. There were so many "Jimmy Chen" shops that one Jimmy Chen advertised his place as "The Original Jimmy Chen," and another "The International Jimmy Chen." One refugee from Canton, May Wong, solved the name problem when she opened her tailor shop across from the Miramar Hotel. Miss Wong put FREEDOM on the front of her shop in red neon lights.

Some energetic refugees became free-lancers—roaming the streets seeking business as "dentists," "medicine men," "barbers," and "letter writers." Other refugees repaired fountain pens, carried sacks of buttons and waited in ambush for tourists with missing buttons, or tediously repaired women's hose by hand. And of course any tourist who stopped to glance at a guidebook was automatically getting a shoeshine.

There were also many refugees who begged until they were arrested. But there were numbers who were qualified to beg but did not want charity. Like Tao Fong, a quadruple amputee who had a wife and four children. Tao had been a guerrilla with the Nationalist army when Japanese soldiers caught him and cut off his feet and hands. Shuffling on stumps, he reached Hong Kong with his family in 1949— they would have been classified as "useless" under Communism—and immediately went into the engraving business. He clamped the object to be engraved in a vise and worked his etching tools with his mouth.

Many small children held full-time jobs in Hong Kong, and the Maryknoll Sisters were well equipped to handle these unfortunate cases. One Sunday, Sister Thomas was strolling through Kowloon's Mo Faan Tsuen village when she was attracted to a six-year-old girl's extremely worried face. The child, Liu Siu Fan, had her five-month-old brother strapped to her back and was caring for the "house" (an 8-by-8-foot hut) and her four other younger brothers and sisters whose ages ranged from a year and a half to five years. Siu Fan's mother and twelve-year-old sister worked in a textile mill at sweatshop wages.

Life, Siu Fan explained softly, hadn't been quite so bad when her father was with them. The family had escaped from Canton, and the father had hawked vegetables until he received word that his brother was desperately ill and wanted to see him. Mr. Liu obtained both a legal entrance and exit permit to China. But the Reds kept him for a labor-camp project.

The Maryknoll Sisters placed Siu Fan's younger brothers and sisters with the Hong Kong Society for the Protection of Children. At the age of six, Siu Fan herself began to learn a trade in Maryknoll's Poor School, which divided its pupils' time between education and employment training. After she recovered from the fright of the huge building—an ordinary schoolroom—and learned what a pencil was and how to hold it, Siu Fan became a very bright student. She also learned enough about sewing gloves to supplement the family income.

Siu Fan's desk was directly across from eleven-year-old Taai Oi Chan, who usually came to school with bloodshot eyes because she had to add to her family's income by assembling plastic roses by lantern light until midnight every night.

Oi Chan's mother sold vegetables in the streets for 35 cents a day. She could not afford both vegetables and a license and was arrested regularly, taken to police stations for three or four hours, and given another warning. She kept fanning out from her home territory to avoid being arrested by the same police and jailed for multiple offenses. Her husband, once a chicken farmer north of Canton, averaged two days of cooliework a week, and the only home they could afford was a tin lean-to.

The Maryknoll Sisters arranged for the Taai children to be cared for while Oi Chan received an education and learned a sewing trade. Like hundreds of benefactors of the Sisters' Poor School, she was soon earning what she considered a fantastic living.

Across from the Poor School is the Sisters' industrial section for older girls too destitute to attend any school. They had to earn all or a substantial part of their family incomes by sewing, embroidering or knitting. The girls usually started in this section at fourteen, without previous formal education, and received 17½ cents a day. After they had learned to sew church vestments to be sold in the United States, the daily wage was raised to $1.05.

The sectional administrator, Sister Maria Teresa, bubbled with enthusiasm as she hustled around the room, advising female workers. Sister Maria Teresa, a Chinese who relinquished considerable wealth when she entered the convent thirty years ago, realized the young employees' problems and knew how to help them.

A case in point, she said, was twelve-year-old Yeung Ngaan, who hemstitched coats. Ngaan's father was a carpenter and her mother a seamstress in a Communist commune in Canton until 1960, when they couldn't bear Communism any longer. The Yeung family obtained a legal exit permit to Hong Kong, and the border guards politely allowed Ngaan, her sister and mother to cross. Then they arrested the father. He was executed later. The girls and their mother made it into Hong Kong, where they moved in with a widowed aunt who supported five children by sewing part time at the Maryknoll industrial plant. Ngaan's mother found a low-paying servant's job, and her fourteen-year-old sister was hired by a textile mill.

Mrs. Yeung was so heartbroken over her husband's fate that she died eight months later. The aunt recommended Yeung Ngaan for the Maryknoll industrial department.

Despite the commotion Ngaan caused by telling her story to an interviewer in the sewing room, a chubby girl standing nearby—seventeen-year-old Hon Wai Fong—never looked up.

Wai Fong refused to discuss her background when Sister Maria Teresa attempted to learn its details. There was a reason for her tight-lipped attitude about the past. In Toishan, China, her father Captain Hon had been an aide to Generalissimo Chiang Kai-shek. Although the Hon family arrived in Hong Kong with $75, which went for a house, no firm would risk giving the Nationalist officer employment. Then a fever left him too ill for cooliework, and in desperation he took a job pasting paper shopping bags together for 5½ cents a day. He never accumulated an extra day's food to enable him to seek higher employment. The wife strung two buckets on a pole and carried water for the same salary. Then Mr. Hon became so weak that he couldn't produce his quota of shopping bags and was fired. He died three weeks later.

Wai Fong, eleven-year-old student in the Poor School at the time, asked to be transferred to the industrial section to supplement the mother's salary. Wai Fong not only worked herself into an 87-cents-a-day sewing position, but also encouraged the Sisters to write her mother a letter of introduction that resulted in a cleaning job. The brother then got a small paying job as a second-rate tailor and sent Wai Fong to a government school.

While Wai Fong's case was being discussed by the Sisters, a golden-haired little girl with skin as white as tissue paper and wearing thick glasses sidled up.

"Hello, my name is Agnes," she proudly announced in English. "I am five years old. How are you?"

"How are you, Agnes?" the Sisters replied.

"Hello, my name is Agnes. I am five years old. How are you?"

Agnes' mother was one of ten women regularly employed to sew elaborate vestments in the Maryknoll industrial section. She had wanted to give Agnes away as a baby because she was an albino—something Chinese despise. The sewer's six other children, including an albino son, helped change her mind. Agnes normally would have been in kindergarten, but this was Ching Ming festival day,[2] and so she stayed in

---

[2] The annual spring day when graves are cleaned and incense and food are offered to the dead.

the workshop, her second home. Agnes' father had escaped from a Communist prison in Canton and smuggled his family to Hong Kong, but the prison ordeal proved too much for him. When strong enough, he earned 10 cents a day assembling plastic toys.

Agnes skipped away and received a playful pat from a thin little sixty-eight-year-old woman who was a sewer. "She started working for our school in 1935," Sister Maria Teresa pointed out, "and came back after the Japanese were gone from here. She's a real good sewer too." The little woman believed in the Christian religion, but unfortunately was unable to be baptized. It would have eliminated a precious job.

This Buddhist woman had a forty-four-year-old blind son who was married and had a small daughter. He was not dependent on charity, because he was a fortuneteller. Every morning the mother set up his little tent in front of the temple and arranged the statues, religious articles and a human skull which he used as a crystal ball. Then she led her son to the tent, started his joss sticks burning, and left him to go to work. If she had joined the Catholic Church, she would not have been alllowed to assemble her son's Buddhist equipment. And she could not see putting anyone out of work in Hong Kong. Her other son had a hard enough time walking the streets trying to find watches to repair.

The Sisters ran a major employment agency. Their King's Park welfare center had 6,200 needy families registered and was supervised by Sister Moira, who spent seven months under Communist house arrest in Wuchow, China. A spare cor-

73

ner of the clinic was rented to a woman who made gloves, and when Sister Moira found anyone desperate for work, this woman hired her to make gloves there or at piece rates at home. This home employment permitted young widows to work and still tend their children.

One typical glovemaker was Mrs. Tak, whose husband had formerly owned a shoe factory in Shanghai. After the Communists confiscated the plant, the Tak family salvaged enough money to buy a dirt-floor hut and a hand-operated shoemaking machine in Hong Kong. Mr. Tak made shoes at home and sold them in the streets until he contracted TB. Then Mrs. Tak was hired to make gloves in the welfare center while he was recuperating. One Friday the Sisters noticed that one of Mrs. Tak's eyes was bloodshot. They gave her some eyewash and suggested she see the nurse. But she had already lost the sight of the eye. Then the Tak baby also got TB, presumably from the father, and Mrs. Tak became ill with a serious malady which the doctors could not diagnose.

Luckily the husband had recovered, and Sister Moira's letter helped him to get a job in the British military barracks. But a theft occurred there and someone had to be punished. Mr. Tak was accused, though steadfastly maintaining his innocence. Nevertheless he was fired, and one does not get a decent job in Hong Kong with that kind of black mark. He hunted in vain for three months. When the theft was investigated thoroughly, the real thief was caught and confessed. Mr. Tak was completely cleared and received an apology from his former employers, but they could not rehire him.

74

His job had been filled by another refugee. Mrs. Tak returned to making gloves.

Another badly needed job went to Mrs. Sze. She walked into Maryknoll clinic, crying. She had, she sobbed, reached the end of the world. Her husband was never able to get any steady work, no matter how hard he tried. She had fed their six children—all under eight years of age—by running a textile machine. But someone had accidentally started her machine while she was oiling it, and the machine had cut off two of her fingers at the first joints. Mrs. Sze received first aid from an unlicensed factory doctor (a common enough practice in Hong Kong), but was not able to operate the machine at full capacity and was dismissed.

"Not only is there nothing for the children to eat tonight," the refugee woman cried, "but nobody will ever hire me for work again. They just shake their heads when they see my hand."

Sister Moira gave her a fifty-pound bag of rice, and Mrs. Sze learned to knit. Within two weeks she was supporting the family by knitting gloves.

If Mrs. Sze had not been able to learn to knit, she could have had employment in the independently operated plastic-flower factory in the rear of the Maryknoll clinic. The Sisters met the proprietor when they baptized his dying baby girl. Later the Sisters made an investment—$1,750—to start him in this industry.[3] He quickly repaid the loan by manufactur-

[3] Along with textiles, the plastic flower-fruit business is Hong Kong's most rapidly growing industry. Utilizing refugees, 239 factories began manufacturing the flowers. The 1960 plastic flower exports totaled $26,250,000 of which $18,550,000 was shipped to the United States. Dull statistics sometimes tell a

ing flower leaves and hiring 200 of the area's needy persons to assemble them at home.

Still, there never will be enough jobs in Hong Kong. As late as 1962, over 200,000 refugees reported that they still had not found any semblance of permanent jobs. And more refugees slip in every night.

---

sensational story: The 1960 exports increased 140 percent over 1959; exports for 1959 increased 800 percent over 1958; and the 1958 exports were a *4,000* percent rise over 1957.

# 7.

## A HELPING HAND

**P**ETER Poon awoke the instant his wife nudged him.

"Three thirty?" He yawned and automatically pulled on his black-cloth shoes.

"Yes," she replied wearily. It was Mrs. Poon's turn to sleep on the bed. With fourteen people calling this 10-by-14-foot shack in Hong Kong's Shek Kip Mei squatter area home, sleeping had to be in shifts.

But this was the schedule Poon needed. It was time to wake Loh, his cousin who owned the hut. Both dashed their faces with water from the same bucket, picked up their straw baskets, and began the mile-and-a-half walk to the wholesale market. Each purchased a basket of cakes, then walked six blocks over to Nga Tsin Long Road, across the Kowloon city market. Soon it would be daylight—time to begin hawking breakfast cakes.

Neither owned a hawker's license nor an expensive 3-by-5-foot seller's stall. Instead, they worked streets adjacent to stalls where people with no home refrigeration bought one meal at a time. With no rent or overhead, they could peddle cakes for less than 2 cents each, underselling shopkeepers.

But Poon and Loh had to be highly aggressive to sell anything. Hawkers' cries maintained a continuous buzz. A government survey had concluded that 5,000 such hawkers were selling to 11,000 people in twenty-five different areas of the neighborhood, not counting the competition from women who made soup and sold it on the streets.

There was usually an onrush of hawkers toward women servants shopping for their employers. Poon always tried to convince these potential customers that his cakes were identical with those of the shopkeepers—only cheaper. The servants, too, could make a penny. A servant generally would buy a half-dozen cakes, which often made Poon's day a successful one.

Salesmanship was not the only skill needed to survive. Of primary importance was catching rumors about a mass raid on unlicensed hawking, or the sight of a hawker-control-force officer demanding a license.

Since Chinese don't buy cakes after mealtime, Poon and Loh stopped selling at 10 A.M., with one keeping the cakes while the other searched for steadier work. Poon usually visited dye factories, textile mills and construction camps. Most places had such long lines that it was obviously foolish to wait. And it didn't make much difference if he was interviewed. With an ulcer, tumor and hernia, Poon couldn't do heavy cooliework. His awkward Hakka dialect presented another obstacle in Hong Kong. There would be an automatic shake of the head when he mentioned his former occupation as "farmer." One foreman said, in a cutting tone, "Does this look like a farm?"

Poon and Loh took an afternoon nap until sundown, when people came out again to buy supper, then sold until midnight. With an average day's sale, they showed a gross profit of 80 cents. They netted 88 cents on extraordinarily good days; a poor day—frequent during typhoon seasons—usually resulted in a 53-cent profit. This daily profit not only clothed and fed fourteen people, but made small payments on the boards and tin they bought to build a shack.

There were no Sundays of rest. Even though Poon had converted from Buddhism to Catholicism, he still had to work on Sundays.

The only deviation from his usually depressing routine was at Christmas in 1953—his first after becoming a Christian. He took his family to church, then discussed the celebrations around the world—particularly in America. He heard a commotion. Maybe, he thought, it was a giant Christmas celebration. No, the man running through the camp warned there was an uncontrollable fire and every house would be gone within an hour. They only had time to gather personal belongings before the fire spread into Hong Kong's most spectacular blaze, destroying 58,000 refugee homes.

The Poons and Lohs finished Christmas night—the first

they had ever celebrated—in Hong Kong's streets. Both government and social workers entered the disaster area, and a Maryknoll Sister, noticing Poon's strange cough, invited him to the clinic and found him a doctor.

The Sister mentioned Poon's predicament to Father Curran, who interviewed him for a job vacancy. The man was not illiterate, the Maryknoll priest observed, but a tragic case of an intelligent man virtually begging. He employed him as the church's handyman, and Poon survived the tenures of two other priests.

Father Dempsey also was impressed by Poon's sincerity, but realized he couldn't continue working without an operation. The priest made hospital arrangements for Poon. After he recovered and moved into a resettlement cottage, he was promoted to a $75-a-month job interviewing charity applicants and weeding out undesirables.

His wife, though, was reluctant to relinquish their cake "franchise." She still sold cakes and bottled water in front of their house, averaging only 50- to 75-cents profit a month. But that paid the government's $2.50 quarterly rent on the cottage land.

"We certainly get seventy-five dollars' worth of work out of him," said Father Dempsey. "He's such a respected and admired man in the community that he has to work overtime. You'd have to say he's more than a community leader. Any time there's an argument, they come to Poon for a settlement. Here was a man who needed only a hand to climb out of the ditch."

In China, Peter Poon had been a Nationalist general. Born

in 1904, he had joined the Chinese army in 1926, been seriously wounded in two civil war battles, and become a major general and second in command to General Law Cheuk Wing of the Nationalist's 19th Route army. He saw combat against the Japanese for eight years around Shanghai and Hankow.

Poon was in battle for nineteen years and came out of World War II a frayed man. He retired, pooled his savings with those of friends who wanted a cooperative investment, and purchased a 290-acre farm near Kiangsi in northwest China. Poon, his wife and eight children ran the farm until the Communists arrested him in 1948, led him to a hearing, checked his money and said everything was going to be O.K. The following morning six soldiers appeared and said he was guilty of "owning land."

Poon and his family were forced to change into their worst clothes, so the People's government could give the newer ones to "the rightful owners." Since Poon had not actually fought the Communists after World War II, he was given the privilege of remaining on the farm—in a shed. They still tended the land, which had been redefined "People's Property," but were given only three ounces of rice daily.

The family was separated; several friends and neighbors were publicly executed by firing squads as examples; relatives went to labor camps and were never heard from again. Poon himself spent seven months in a labor camp, but his food ration was reduced when he wasn't capable of as much work as stronger men. The cadre leader had a work quota, and

81

when Poon applied to return to his native Canton, he obligingly approved. The family, meanwhile, had safely reached Hong Kong and arranged for Cousin Loh to smuggle him small amounts of meal money. Poon skipped a meal a day until he saved enough for the ninety-mile train ride to Lowu, where he was allowed into Hong Kong.

General Poon was mannerly, but appeared frightened when he first sat at Father Dempsey's kitchen table for an interview. He volunteered no information; he answered questions cautiously.

Poon was thanked for his time—the time, he was told, of a general. His eyes shimmered, as if he suddenly remembered that he had once been important. Then he sat back and fondled the salt-and-pepper shakers.

"Do you know how bad Communism in China?" he said, pointing out the window at a cottage. "Mrs. Lee there teaches at Maryknoll school. I knew her and her husband in China. He was sent to Siberia and never heard from again. Communism will never succeed in China, I know. People at point now—and I hear from them—where they don't care to live any more as the slaves they are. Nothing but fear, pressure, terror, and starvation. Never met one person in favor of it. Communist Party getting weaker. Someday a third party will come along and we can return to our country. Chiang Kai-shek could overtake them now and liberate the country. Now is the time. I tell you the military would escape if they could."

China's landlords found the transition from being wealthy to begging in Hong Kong a laborious adjustment. Profes-

sional men's knowledge allowed them to retain a slight out-
line of inward self-respect, no matter how low they sank.
The landlord's lifetime accomplishment, however, had been
his property, and he had had to run from it like a criminal.

One such prey was Tsang Wai Meng, who was born in
1913 near Rangoon, and moved with his two brothers to
Hengling, China. They purchased a piece of land that annually produced 200 bushels of rice, rented it, then worked in
shops. They reinvested the small profits in additional land. It
was such a wicked offense, a Communist cadre decided to
give the Tsangs a "public trial." It was the same act. Wai
Meng's two brothers and their wives were tied and led to the
town square, and the people ordered to crowd around. Then
the cadre boss who portrayed the judge announced the crime:
"Guilty of owning the People's land! What shall we do with
them? What is the wish of the people?"

The usual Communist agents mingling in the crowd yelled,
"Kill them, kill them! They deserve to die."

"Then," the judge decreed, "it is the wish of the people
that you must die for your crimes."

Tsang Wai Meng, his wife and six children were forced
to witness it—his two brothers and their wives were lined
against their own barn and shot.

In February 1951, the remaining Tsang slipped his family
out of that area and left for Hong Kong, saying he would
send for them when he got a job. He had not found employment by August, and the family could wait no longer. They
reached Hong Kong without difficulty. Hong Kong itself
was the difficulty. A bespectacled man of 5 foot 4, Tsang

had dropped to seventy-eight pounds when his family arrived. He was surviving on friends' handouts until they tired of him. His means of support consisted of about 10 percent cooliework and 90 percent begging. The family slept in the streets.

One November day Tsang wandered into Father Trube's hillside reading room-clinic. Speaking Hakka, which Father Trube understood, the refugee asked, "Are you church man? Christian. Catholic?"

"I'm a Catholic priest," Father Trube replied.

"I not belong," he said, in a squeaky tone, "but I know something about them. Your church stood up and fight the Communists. They know about your church in Rangoon too."

Here was someone hungry for food and knowledge. Father Trube handed him one of his lunch sandwiches, and he ate it like a desperate man. Then he proceeded to explain that he could make chairs out of rattan. In fact he had once done a little of that in Rangoon—even had made a couple here in Hong Kong for a middleman at a profit of 35 cents. But that took all day, sometimes more than a day, and he couldn't even eat, let alone find a roof for his family.

Father Trube had a proposition for him. He could attend Maryknoll's three-week course in rattan furniture-making and he could sleep on the floor of the school and have a meal a day. Father Trube found some families willing to take in the wife and children each day for three weeks.

"This will be an investment," Father Trube said. "An investment in you."

84

After Tsang learned to make marketable chairs, Father Trube allowed him to remain in the school. He also gave the family enough rice for a month. They made chairs in Chiu Pen Sun Street for three months, finally accumulating enough money for a home. Once out of the street, the family turned out three chairs a day and peddled them to middlemen. Occasionally Father Trube found Tsang and other students some contacts that eliminated the middleman's profit. All five sons were making chairs—so fast that three months later Tsang asked Father Trube if another graduate wanted to help him. Tsang obtained a small loan on his hut to acquire more rattan, and six months later had five Maryknoll graduates working for him in front of his home.

A year later he bought a small, four-story factory near the Walled City and moved into the top floor. Nine months later he opened a store catering to tourists on fashionable Nathan Road. The following year he purchased another factory and was manufacturing 5,000 rattan chairs—plus handbags and baskets—a month. He could make 10,000 chairs monthly if he could sell them.

Most of his employees have either been graduates of the Maryknoll course or poor refugees. Maryknoll eventually discontinued the furniture school, but Tsang's factory and extracurricular activities took up the slack. He donated part of his profits to a club to help newly escaped refugees from his Hengling district. Moreover, if they wanted to make chairs for a living, they were paid while they learned and guaranteed regular employment when they mastered the trade.

Tsang, though, has one strict factory rule. Although he hires mostly poor people, he has only the definite requirement that they be bitterly anti-Communist. He checks, and has the workers double check, to be sure that no member of a Communist union ever gets into his place.

A Communist union leader once tried to persuade Tsang's group to defect to his Red Union.

"The men here have a free union," Tsang said. "Why should they be crazy enough to join a slave union?"

Tsang is an extremely proud man—proud of his family and his new religion. He returns to Bishop Ford Center regularly to donate furniture or Christmas toys, or to inquire if anyone needs a job badly. Discussing his past, he whipped out one of his calling cards, plus postcards from a son who had graduated from the University of California and was working on a master's degree at Santa Barbara.

"See." He chuckled, flashing a mimeographed program in English which he couldn't read. His son had played the Chinese flute at an international student gathering in California. Another pocket contained pictures of his other sons —one at the Jesuits' Wah Yan College in Hong Kong, another in middle school, and two others in Maryknoll's Bishop Ford School.

After finishing a lengthy story of each son, Tsang dove into his next favorite subject: Communism.

"If Communist fight the good people in streets tomorrow in Hong Kong," he began, "they would be outnumbered one hundred to one. When you ever see or experience Communism, see family and friends executed, you don't want any part of it. People who recently escape tell me they steal from government at night. Have to. The soldiers lose control near Ha Wah city. They overpower soldiers and cadres to get something to eat, but next day a new army comes in and machine-guns into the village for revenge. Kill hundreds of people. People wait ten to twelve years now, and they all ask me soon as they escape—also some in secret letters— 'When Chiang Kai-shek coming back?' They rise up by millions with stones and shovels. Soldiers could not machine-gun them fast enough. If Chiang Kai-shek let me know when he make landing, I can personally get three villages to revolt against Communists."

"The guy's saying a lot, isn't he?" Father Trube was asked.

"It's cases like his that are my most rewarding experiences," Father Trube replied. "Just a small loan and some new knowledge to get him on his feet, and he's repaid it a thousand times in gifts. Maybe more. Oh, you mean about his getting three villages to revolt? Don't doubt him. When he got a start, he put the same spirit into making chairs in the streets."

# 8.

## THE MEDICINE MEN

**T**WO percent of the refugees arrived in Hong Kong with tuberculosis, resulting in over a hundred deaths a week. Uncounted thousands soon had diphtheria, typhoid fever, chickenpox, malaria and bacillary dysentery. There was no *status quo* among the healthy. It was almost expected that a squatter would contact a communicable disease or develop beriberi.

Without sanitation facilities, refugees poured human waste over one side of a sampan and dipped on the other for drinking water. Squatters used the same water before sufficient public faucets and latrines were installed. The hungry who scrounged garbage cans for food scraps couldn't consider sanitation. They ate shellfish from the slimy waters of sewer outlets, although they were known to be infectious.

88

The Chinese are habitually a clean race, but their crowded, primitive conditions nullified any individual precautions. Disease spread through the streets with the wandering refugees. There was only one starkly obvious answer—more medical facilities. Before the refugee deluge, the Hong Kong government had recognized an alarming hospital shortage. Now it was an uncontrollable predicament.

An additional complication was Hong Kong's firm regulations forbidding anyone to practice medicine, regardless of background, unless they were graduates of the University of Hong Kong or another British institution. This not only eliminated the Maryknoll Fathers and other volunteers, but most of the Chinese doctors who had left the mainland. Simple humanitarianism caused Maryknoll to cut corners in desperate situations. Only the Communists,[1] who ventured into unions, industry, schools, banks and newspapers, carefully adhered to the medical rule.

The Maryknoll Fathers found a loophole. They were allowed to operate clinics at each of the four parishes, provided they were staffed by registered trained nurses. And the Sister doctors and nurses expelled from China were highly qualified, though they had few facilities or supplies. "At first," the priests recalled, "we only had a bunch of odds-and-ends pills to pass out."

But anything was an improvement. And in the same manner that they solicited jobs and donations, Maryknoll priests contacted doctors and urged them to donate a few evening

[1] After the Cannossian Sisters worked night and day on their floating clinic in Aberdeen Bay to save a refugee man, the Communists kidnapped him and took him back to China.

hours at their clinics. Additionally, the Sisters launched an accelerated sanitation and hygiene program and attempted to catch the diseases in their early stages. For example, tuberculosis isn't considered too serious in America if detected early. The Chinese usually learned they had TB when they were dying, and even if there was hospital space in Hong Kong, there was a policy against hopeless cases.

Shots in the arm had gained a fairy-tale reputation in China's Kwangtung and Kwangsi provinces, primarily from work pioneered by Maryknoll and Protestant hospital staffs. Unlike Dr. Tom Dooley's initial problem in North Vietnam, where natives were brainwashed into believing inoculations were poison, the Chinese continued to love shots. Even children who fought against taking vitamin capsules to combat beriberi developed a toylike fondness for needles. Five- and six-year-old tousle-haired youngsters grinned broadly— like American children at Christmas—as they eagerly rolled up their sleeves.

"I can't recall an incident nor ever heard of anyone balking on their shots at our clinics," said Father Edmonds. Where Americans draw in their breath at the sting of the shot, the Chinese give the appearance of enjoying it. The pain means the needle is going in and represents a sensational Western magic. "It's not the medicine," they argue, "but the needle."

The older patients had the same attitude. When nurses at Our Lady of Maryknoll Hospital [2] asked the nature of their

---

[2] The hospital, opened in 1962, was built as part of the World Refugee Year program, and every piece of equipment—secondhand dentist chairs, bedpans, sample medicines—was donated by Americans. It is staffed by ten medical nuns

ailments, many responded by saying, *"Ta cham."* ("Stick needle.")

Even the Communists wanted shots. And Monsignor John Romaniello obliged all the needy in his Kweilin diocese. "Although the kids were being brainwashed into Communists," he said, "they nevertheless were grateful. Until Communist authorities issued a bulletin: 'Sure the American missioner's medicine is good. It heals your body and poisons your mind at the same time. They want you to die in a few years.'" After that some of the young guards who had smiled, saluted and tipped their caps as they passed only stared coldly.

But the general popularity of vaccination continued to a point where it almost became a problem in itself. Many of the sick stalked away peevishly if they could not have shots, refusing to believe that pills or liquid medicine were capable of producing the same results.

But men like Mr. Teck, who made shoes in the streets, helped change that opinion. He returned to the hospital three times, refusing to see anyone but the particular Sister who had treated him before. "Oh, I not sick today." He grinned. "I come back to report that the brown medicine in a bottle is a success and will work. It is O.K. to give the people here. I will tell everyone I see."

Many like Mr. Teck gained such assurance that they became amateur doctors themselves. If they had surplus medicine, they voluntarily treated anyone they heard was sick, for free. A coolie rushed to a neighbor suffering from a badly mashed hand and poured the remains of his cough syrup over

and has seventy-five beds and an outpatient clinic. It charges according to income. The standard registration fee—if they have it—is 17 cents.

the wound. "I guarantee this to work," he said convincingly. "I so sick I couldn't talk, but it heal me."

It was not the amateur doctor that aggravated Maryknoll's problem. It was the "professional." The Chinese medicine man. At one time Chinese herb medicine far exceeded the civilized world's remedies; their *Book of the Internal* was written 3,000 years ago, and their folklore celebrates the physician who bravely tasted herbs to discover medical secrets. Some herbs were known to stop infection a thousand years before the discovery of penicillin. The trouble is, there has been little progress in the last 1,000 years.

Though the medicine man's practice isn't as busy as in the "good old days," he is far from nonexistent. Father Michael McKiernan, who succeeded Father Jim Smith as Maryknoll's Hong Kong superior in 1958, volunteered to show "just how far we have to go." Particularly since the Maryknoll headquarters was only a five-minute walk from Stanley village's "medicine row." The priest had to weave in and out of men playing mah-jongg, and around women cooking in the narrow streets, to reach the outdoor "apothecary shops."

The most common remedy—a kind of Chinese equivalent of Bufferin—was entire chickens, feathers and internals included, soaked in a white rice wine. Other popular drugs included chicken feet, cats, monkeys and snakes aged in rich wine. Some prescriptions, recommended only for certain ailments under particular phases of the moon, were dried snakes mixed with orange peel; a blend of animal horn and lizard teas; and powdered pearl and ginseng. All formulas are secret, motivated by the ancient Chinese theory: "Teach the student too much and there soon will be no room for the teacher."

The medicine men solemnly attempt anything short of a brain operation. One old-timer in the Walled City had a consistent record of discrediting Western practices and increasing hospital business. A twelve-year-old boy slipped on a roof he was repairing and broke his elbow. The medicine man massaged the socket until the protective coating was rubbed away. The arm automatically stiffened, and the boy's mother brought him to the Bishop Ford Center. He was sent to Dr. Fong, a bone specialist. "We'll have to wait a year for the bone to stop growing," the doctor pointed out. A year later Dr. Fong chipped away the bone mass, made a new joint, and after another year's steady exercise, was able to restore the arm to 75 percent normal use.

Some medicine men are versatile. But their herbs only irritated further the sixty-five-year-old man who had been blind for years from cataracts. Finally, in February of 1962, Father Trube arranged for him to use the cornea bank at a government hospital. When the day for admission arrived, the old-timer panicked.

"Now there isn't a thing in the world to be afraid of," Father Trube cautioned.

"But I am scared, Father," he replied, "real scared. I'm not afraid of the doctor, but what if he puts in blue eyes?"

"No, I guarantee it won't happen," the priest said. "I'll go down and pick out brown eyes for you."

The operation was successful. The old man looked around, grinned, then demanded a mirror to verify the fact that he had brown eyes. Later he excitedly climbed the steep Bishop

Ford Center hill to thank the priest. "Your face," he said, "looks exactly like I thought it would by the way you talk."

Despite all the free medical help, many refugees never received even a Band-Aid, and were so desperate they considered themselves fortunate if they could afford a medicine man. A forty-year-old woman named Kwong—whose husband had been shot and killed as they were escaping China—staggered into Hong Kong alone and penniless. But because her cancer was in an incurable, advanced stage, she was ineligible for treatment in a government hospital.

Mrs. Kwong was offered a solution. All she had to do was sell this white powder, heroin, and if she sold enough she could pay for an operation. If she was arrested, the government would automatically send her to Queen Mary Hospital for the necessary surgery so she could serve her short prison sentence. She had no alternative. She was caught, all right, and confined to the prison infirmary.

One day Mrs. Kwong met Sister Teresa during the Maryknoller's weekly visit to the prison, and the Sister began talking religion. Mrs. Kwong was a pagan who had never heard of Christianity, but learned the doctrine and was converted. Then she began telling the woman in the next bed—who was also in on dope charges and dying of cancer—how peaceful she felt about dying. Her only problem, she persisted, was that her sentence was due to expire and she would have to leave the prison. She died the day her three-month term ended.

The other patient, who had listened to the religious' instructions, was so impressed with the peacefulness of Mrs.

Kwong's death that she asked to be instructed too, and was baptized by Sister Joan Catherine.

Another problem in Hong Kong is pregnancy. Since many Chinese women think nothing of having a baby on a Tuesday afternoon and returning to work on Wednesday, there are many complications with later births. Some women lose all of their children, and the Chinese consider a childless home such a calamity that the well-to-do buy babies. Others install heaters in their homes "to give warmth to the family"—to use the Chinese expression.

Father Trube cited a typical pregnancy ailment one day when he saw a little boy leaving the school. "That kid is some story," the priest began. "This pregnant woman had been married fifteen years and all seven of her babies had been stillborn. She was pregnant again, and her husband said he had decided to leave her for another woman. We arranged for her to see Dr. Christine Chow. She was X-rayed for the child's position and received the necessary treatment. That was the little boy—he's seven now. He has a brother and a sister too."

Maternity cases also occupy much of the time of Sister Ignatia, Administrator of Our Lady of Maryknoll Hospital which is off Shatin Pass Road and overlooks a resettlement area of 500,000 people.

One instance involved a Hakka woman whom Sister Ignatia had known in Kaying. Her husband, a weaver, openly despised her for remaining barren during their sixteen years of marriage, but when she had an extreme pain, he showed a change of heart and contacted a Chinese doctor. The doctor said she was dying of cancer. The Chinese contend that evil spirits prohibit anyone from dying in a rented house, so the woman asked Sister Ignatia for a place in which to die. Her husband had saved $35, but insisted he couldn't "waste it on an operation." He had to "buy himself a baby."

The Sisters got her the operation—for a spinal condition, not cancer—and she recovered completely and had two healthy children.

"These are the kind of cases we run into on the streets every day," Sister Ignatia said, "One woman—and we didn't know each other—was evidently in horrible pain. So was her baby. I started talking to her, and she said nobody could help her. She said they were both dying. She was correct, too. They had hookworm, were anemic, and needed transfusions. We treated them, and now they are both perfectly healthy. She's working too. It's as all the other Sisters say. The children just haven't eaten, and a handful of vitamins taken according to instructions actually puts the majority in normal condition."

Maryknoll Sisters are trying to combat the high infant mortality rate with baby sections in their clinics. The 200 daily patients range from those needing simple preventive salves to cases such as the baby Lee girl.

The child, the seventh in the family, weighed only three pounds at birth and gained just one ounce in three months. Sisters Monica Marie and Thomas Ann detected a serious ailment which prevented the flow of milk. After treatment the baby gained a full pound in the next month.

Lowu Bridge, separating sprawling Communist China (background) from the cramped British colony of Hong Kong, where 1,500,000 Chinese have fled from Red tyranny to start a new life.

Chinese refugees crowded into makeshift shanties, but Maryknoll has founded community centers, like the large white structure at the right, to alleviate their suffering.

Discarded crates, driftwood and scraps became the materials that many desperate Chinese squatters used to build tiny shelters in overcrowded Hong Kong.

Within a few hours, this fire devastated an entire Hong Kong refugee village. More than 2,000 buildings were destroyed, nine died, and 24,000 were rendered homeless.

Children search the ruins of their homes after fire swept a squatter settlement on Christmas Eve, 1953, leaving 50,000 homeless.

With generous donors behind them, the Maryknoll Fathers and Sisters began a low-cost housing plan for the homeless refugees. These granite structures, set in cement, are fireproof.

The Maryknoll school-chapel founded by Father Howard Trube

One of the many new fireproof dwellings Maryknoll has built for refugees whose wooden huts were destroyed by fire. Cost of these new "mansions"— about $122.

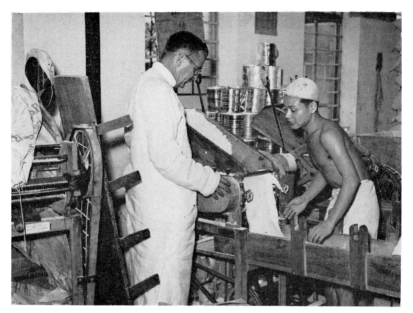

Father Howard Trube, the first Maryknoll missionary to live and work among the refugees, supervises the processing of American surplus food.

Father Arthur Dempsey, who began a weaving cooperative and taught refugees new trades, holds a class in typing. Graduates are then found jobs in Hong Kong.

Father Trube stages programs for youngsters to prevent them from falling into juvenile delinquency. One sixth of Hong Kong's population belongs to secret, criminal societies. It was Father Trube who helped stop the infamous "Fourteen K" gang's robberies and blackmailing.

Father Stephen Edmonds' clinic provides medical care for refugees.

Monsignor John Romaniello, whose work has saved thousands from starvation.

Most refugees had no facilities for using surplus flour, so Monsignor Romaniello found the solution by making noodles from hand-cranked machines. The noodles, which dry quickly in the warm Hong Kong sun, became a sensation among the hungry refugees.

During a trip to Hong Kong, Attorney General Robert Kennedy helps Monsignor Romaniello distribute packages of noodles to refugees.

Maryknoll's baby clinic serves a dual purpose. The Sisters have a nursery branch which charges working mothers 3 ½ cents a day to care for children. "Actually they get more food than that," explained Sister Moira, "but this prevents the mothers from feeling they're getting charity, and at the same time allows us to watch their health. When the kids—usually about four years old—come here, their eyes turn on like lights. They eat four or five bowls of rice instead of the normal one to one and a half. They think, of course, that there might never be any more, but after they're here a couple of days, they drop to the normal amount."

Maryknoll can't save every life. There was Mrs. Lau, whose husband was an incurable opium smoker. She peddled preserved fish to feed her three babies. When Mrs. Lau learned that she was dying of cancer, all that worried her was getting the children adopted in a good home.

About that time Sister Ignatia received a request from a Chicago Chinese family named Ching to adopt a "little Chinese girl." She wrote that "three darling children were available." Mrs. Ching answered that they could adopt two, but that three would be out of the question. That provoked her husband into an argument. "And break up a family of three little children?" he snapped. The Chings sent a night letter agreeing to adopt all three.

But even with the Chings' good intentions and the dying mother's request, the Sisters couldn't release the children until they found the father.

Mrs. Lau managed to whisper where her husband Ah Hung might be loafing. "Sometimes," she said, "I heard he goes by the typhoon shelter." He wasn't there, but eventually they found him in a Wanchai district doorway. They got him into court at 9 A.M. to sign the papers.

"Then our troubles started all over again," Sister Ignatia said. "He kept smoking—dope, I guess—and every five minutes he wanted to leave. This went on until the noon lunch bell rang and court was recessed. He said, 'That's it, I'm leaving.' So I said, 'Sit down and keep smoking, will you? Keep smoking, you hear me!'

"I ran up to the desk and said, 'Now look. I've chased this heroin smoker for months and he's going to leave and you'll be putting three little children in the streets.' So the bailiff turned around and we got the papers signed."

The children, a ten-year-old boy and eight- and four-year-old girls, visited the mother at Precious Blood Hospital the day they left for America. Mrs. Lau told the Sisters: "I must hold on until I receive the first letter from America telling me that my children got there safely and are happy in their new home."

"After she started receiving letters regularly," Sister Ignatia said, "she seemed to make a remarkable recovery. In fact she lived three months longer than the doctors predicted and died very peacefully."

Maryknoll centers were able to help the medical situation by actually putting some doctors back in practice. "There's one physician particularly," said Father Trube, "who was desperate when he arrived in Hong Kong. He was a highly respected and honored doctor in China, and it isn't easy for a man of this caliber to accept being disbarred. He was genuinely dedicated, and we used him as a clinic technician. He found this a springboard for reviewing his medical knowledge, passed the government examination, and eventually got his license. When we have a bad case and no money, he gladly helps us out free."

Only a fraction of the Chinese doctors have been this lucky, and most of them did not foresee difficulties in Hong Kong. Wong Cheung Ming, born in 1915 near Canton, had a medical degree from Tokyo's Waseda University and was typical. Wong, with his wife and four children, remained in Kwangsi practicing medicine during the civil war. A week before the Communists marched into his town, he learned that doctors were interned and their wives must scrounge for their own livings. So in July of 1949, he had his savings of $3,000 in Nationalist money—only a few dollars on the international exchange—took the Canton train to Lowu, and bought a one-room house next door to a Fanling bean market. "This will just be temporary," he told his wife, "until I get started in Hong Kong."

Wong took the local train into Kowloon and soon learned that newly arriving doctors had no more status than desperate coolies. Especially if the physicians didn't speak English. He didn't. He applied for jobs every day for two months and couldn't get a single day's work.

Finally, through a friend, Wong got a salesman's job, working on commission for a medical firm. He built the family a "mansion"—26 by 17 feet—and things weren't so bad. Then the medical firm folded. Then his wife died.

99

Father Dempsey heard about Wong's situation through his children, interviewed him, and hired him at $73.75 a month as school secretary. While Father Dempsey was very pleased with Wong's work, the priest realized that his employee regarded it as only a temporary job.

Wong, a good-looking, well-groomed man, discussed his situation while sitting on the steps of Father Dempsey's office. Although he didn't speak English and talked through an interpreter, he watched every word written down in English on the yellow pad.

"All this in Hong Kong is just temporary," he began slowly. "In perhaps a year or a little more I will be practicing medicine again in China. China will be free then. The Communists have broken every rule, every custom, every freedom, and the government is falling apart so fast that it cannot last much longer. Every person who escapes now says this is the time for Chiang Kai-shek to liberate China.

"I hear from doctors inside who smuggle out letters. They're always saying, 'How could anyone be doctor and encourage their own people to die?' People who are weak or over sixty-five are not allowed medicine unless it is smuggled in from Hong Kong or Macao. They are told just give the people something they think is medicine. They are making streptomycin out of sulphur. Other stuff not better than sawdust. See what happened when the cholera break out. About everybody in one village die. Government says, 'More people die, the less there is to feed.' I hope to help when I return."

Another Chinese doctor whom Maryknoll had helped regain his medical license finished up his charity work at the clinic one evening and discussed the China medical situation. "Unless you've actually practiced there, you have no idea what it's like," he said. "Look, now, please don't write down my name. My family in China would suffer. Don't even put down area—they'll know who it is. But I was ordered by the government to always take my own food when I went on trips to visit the seriously ill. It was, of course, my only choice, because there is no food anywhere; people are starving. Do you know that I made thirty-five trips to visit and never got to eat a bite of the food? I was always robbed. That's how hungry people are. Anyway, there wasn't much I could do, even if I found the sick. There just isn't any medicine for the lower classes in China. In fact there is such a low respect for life—the only thing that matters is the Communist members and soldiers—that many doctors were told it is better for the country to let lowly workers die than waste efforts sending them to a hospital. Even then—more so now—I find that medical knowledge is very slight in China. Most time in medical school is spent working in fields, like reforesting areas, and listening to propaganda."

Another refugee doctor who donated his services at Father Edmonds' Chai Wan clinic, graduated from medical school before the Communist take-over and had a sound medical background. He had been assigned to a labor camp and was not allowed to tell a patient his condition regardless of its seriousness. One day a seventeen-year-old boy collapsed

while laying railroad ties. The doctor found he had a 103°
temperature and sent a note to the work leader to excuse the
patient from manual labor "at least for today." The Communist boss, fearing that his production quota might be
lowered slightly, ordered the boy re-examined by another
physician. Meanwhile the first doctor had given the boy
aspirin, and his temperature was naturally lower the next day.
Not only was the sick boy returned to work, but the first
doctor was reported as "a common criminal for seriously
damaging the progress of the People's Republic." The only
way the doctor could remove this blot, he was told, would
be to have fewer illnesses among the labor gangs. Which
meant not reporting them.

Even though permitted to practice, like most he could
sustain no faith or inspiration in his work under such conditions, and headed for Hong Kong with his relatives. Two
of them were shot to death by Communist security police
as they approached the Shumchun River banks.

Still, the Hong Kong Communists work hard at recruit-
ing overseas Chinese doctors for the mainland. One such
doctor in Indonesia succumbed to the blandishment that
he could "safely bring his life savings and family of seven
to his home town and retain the high style of living to
which he had been accustomed." All he had to do, they
promised, was "accept the directorship of a large China hospital, thereby doing a great service for his country." The
physician accepted and did indeed have more liberties than
most Chinese. In fact he was able to return to Indonesia

with his family. But he was so disturbed by the inhuman state of medicine in China that he wrote to the newspapers, exposing the situation, then he and his family committed suicide.

A twenty-seven-year-old doctor from Kwangsi province was granted an exit permit to visit his sick mother who lived across from the public water taps at Bishop Ford Center. He wanted to stay in Hong Kong, but a few days before his permit lapsed he received word that a Communist officer would execute his father if he did not return.

Before returning, he watched a doctor at work in Maryknoll's Bishop Ford clinic. "I feel like a beginning student," he told the priest. "Most of my class time was spent on matters unrelated to medicine. Besides having to spend the greater part of our time working in the field, most of the remaining periods were spent downgrading the 'Imperialist U.S.A. and the Paper Tiger.' For weeks at a time about the only mention of medicine was lectures on how our problem had been increased by the U.S. using Hong Kong as a base for dispatching cholera germs into China."

The Communist technique of propagandizing cholera outbreaks instead of imposing quarantine restrictions or combatting them, has placed additional work on Hong Kong. In August 1961, a cholera epidemic spread through China's Kwangtung province, and the Communists had little more than ground roots and sulphur with which to treat it. There were reports that at least 30,000 died and that the Communists blamed the epidemic on American germ-warfare tactics, as they had during the Korean war. Communist cadres put bodies on display to stimulate the mass meetings. Two fishermen who contracted cholera, however, didn't believe the charges, escaped by boat to the nearby Portuguese colony of Macao, then were smuggled into Hong Kong. The island was set for a cholera epidemic. *Kok lon* (cholera) is a particularly dreaded disease, since it quickly dehydrates the victim. Just dropping the word in the right place can produce wholesale panic.

Maryknoll and other volunteer agencies helped the Hong Kong government to bring the disease under control quickly by inoculating with serum contributed by American military installations and other Southeast Asian countries. The young assistants, Fathers Eugene Thalman and John J. Sullivan, announced over parish public-address systems that inoculations were available, while lay workers walked through the area with portable bullhorns. With the assistance of American and British volunteers and the Catholic Women's League, over 20,000 inoculations were given within thirty-six hours. There were only 2 cholera cases, resulting in 1 death, from the entire area. All together, the seven Maryknoll clinics estimate they gave 100,000 shots. Other agencies brought this total to 1,200,000—or 80 percent of the refugee population—and only 15 deaths from cholera resulted in the entire colony.

Neither Maryknoll nor Protestant workers could have carried out such a program completely without generous American donations and the $50,000 annual medical aid that the United States Government gives both Maryknoll and Lutheran World Service. "Much of this money goes for hospital cases and operations," explained Father Mc-Kiernan, "when we can't find a specialist to take a charity case. There's only one alternative. The sooner you can put a man back on his feet, the sooner he can return to work."

"Much of the goodwill generated here by the American government," said Father Dempsey, "has been the medical aid program. Even though it's only a tiny part of its foreign aid budget."

The results the United States receives from this $50,000 annual grant, when contrasted, for example, with the $2½ billion lavished on Laos, motivates people to shake their heads. There was understandable shock when Robert Aylward, Director of the Refugee and Migration Unit in the American Consulate in Kong Kong, informed the Maryknoll and Lutheran directors that all medical aid would cease at the end of 1962. Both organizations appealed strongly to the U.S. State Department's Office of Refugees and Migration Affairs. A typical appeal was the following letter, dated February 2, 1962, written by Father McKiernan to Director Richard Brown:

> Last year there were 258,700 cases treated in the seven clinics of the Maryknoll Fathers. These people cannot obtain medical help elsewhere ... unless they borrow at 35 to 50 percent interest rates, and then it is impossible to get back on their feet. . . .
>
> Many of the 50,000 refugees who arrive each year need medical care, and it is available to them in areas where they live. It is not necessary for them to spend bus fare to town, a

big factor to a man who earns six Hong Kong dollars [$1.05] a day.... As I understand it, the American Consulate is reluctant to continue this program because: (1) it might become permanent; (2) it does not give them flexibility in allocating funds.... The program has been going on for several years. We fully realize that if there is no money available, the aid will stop. If the money is available for refugees, however, then we would like to see it spent where it does the greatest amount of good for the greatest amount of refugees. Our medical programs do just that.

Secondly, the idea that this program does not leave the Refugee and Migration Unit any flexibility is wide of the mark. Both the medical programs come to U.S. $100,000, which is less than 10 percent of the total amount allocated for this area. I really don't think that an earmarked 10 percent of any amount freezes one's flexibility in administering the total sum. I feel the purpose of American aid is to help the refugees in the best possible manner, and not to insure flexibility for the officers administering it. To change these programs to some other programs would seem like asking a man at the race track not to bet on a horse that had been winning constantly for him because this doesn't give him flexibility in betting!

Mr. Brown's reply stated that: "It was never intended that the Far East Refugee Program would participate permanently in the operations of the refugee installations... It was hoped that it would stimulate public and private organizations to support and expand these FERP-sponsored activities... The success of this approach is exemplified by refugee housing."

Since Hong Kong's refugee housing is entirely subsidized by the British Government, it appears that the United States has, in effect, told the Hong Kong government to "support and expand" the medical programs of the American volunteer relief agencies for Chinese refugees.

Concurrently the State Department gave Haiti, which is not a member of the Alliance for Progress in Latin America, $30 million in aid for a "second chance." There were regular news reports about foreign aid money mysteriously disappearing in Haiti. Nobody seemed to know where it had gone. And the United States has given several billion dollars to Yugoslavia, which is a Communist country. Then a $2 million *monthly* donation was deposited in the Laos account only hours after that country had formed an alleged "neutral" government and assigned the premiership to a Communist who publicly denounced the United States for "vicious warmongering atrocities in Southeast Asia." The downtrodden Hong Kong Chinese, who had been receiving $100,000 annually for medicine and hospitalization, had given the West a bargain propaganda victory. And at a negligible fee.

Hong Kong Communists have been handed another propaganda device—"Who holds life cheaply now?"

# 9.

# THE VICTIMS

MRS. Tsat Loi Fung—or number 5332—was a 1962 benefactor of American medical aid through Maryknoll. The little woman was thirty-seven years old and looked fifty-seven; she was barefoot and wore black coveralls which were too short and had two extra large pockets to carry the goods she peddled. Like most Orientals who love calling cards as introductions, Mrs. Tsat wanted to give the American visitor her "card." It was her Hong Kong identity stamp and peddler's license tied to her coverall loops. She borrowed an ink pad from Sister Maria Petra and stamped the American's notebook with Chinese characters. Then she shook hands left-handedly. She had no right hand.

Mrs. Tsat's family had always been very poor. They

owned and farmed a few yards of land in a low area near Tsang Shing village in Kwangtung province. No one else wanted the land; it flooded every year and they had to remove all their belongings during the high water.

"Flood got as high as me," the four-foot-seven woman explained.

"But we do very good," she continued in Cantonese. "My husband's parents very old, so they live with us. We very well to do. Even have own washbasin to wash our faces and hands in. But even Communists take that. They said, for the government."

The Tsats raised 300 catties [1] of rice a year, which was enough for them to survive on. The farm was so remotely located that the government didn't consider merging it into a commune, and the local cadre made an exception and allowed the Tsats to keep the land. This generous gesture would be repaid with an annual delivery of 200 catties of rice to the government collector. The rice they had been saving for Mrs. Tsat's operation was the first installment.

Her right hand had been shattered by a Japanese bomb during World War II, and now, years later, pieces of flesh were beginning to drop off. With the rice proposition gone, she turned to the husband's distant cousin, who stopped the decay with a herb formula.

The two-thirds reduction in food made the entire family unhealthy. Mrs. Tsat wasn't getting enough nourishment when she was pregnant. A boy baby died three days after

[1] A Communist catty is 1½ pounds.

birth; twin girls were born dead. The children who survived birth soon were near death. The eight-year-old daughter's throat had such a large lump in it that she was unable to talk, and the three-month-old son was deformed by malnutrition.

Finally, in April of 1959, Mrs. Tsat begged the Communist rice official for permission to see a government doctor. She not only was pregnant again, but now boils covered her body.

The Communist wrote a generous prescription. Translated, it meant, "Go Hong Kong." It was an exit permit allowing her to leave the country, but not allowing her to return until she and the children were completely cured.

Mrs. Tsat arrived in Hong Kong without money or contacts, but found a job carrying wood. She saved enough to start hawking green beans. Her earnings were sufficient to support the children, but not herself too. She heard that Maryknoll gave two-pound food bags to needy cases.

A Sister noticed her trying to wiggle the paper sack into the back pack in which she carried the baby. Her "good" hand was black and becoming gangrenous. She had, she said, consulted a Chinese herb doctor because his fee was cheap and the identical treatment had "cured" the decay in the other hand. But this doctor spread the infection.

A shipment of sample Unguentine had arrived the same day. The Sister nurse cleaned and smeared the hand with it. Then as she also discovered the boils and swabbed them, the spunky little woman explained her children's plight. The daughter had had an operation in a Hong Kong government hospital, but was growing weaker.

"She now more sick than ever," Mrs. Tsat told the nurse. "But hospital not allow her to come back second time."

A Sister went home with Mrs. Tsat to see the daughter. She was lying in their rented lean-to, which was against a garage in Homantin's 16th district and for which Mrs. Tsat paid $2.31 a month.

The Sisters used some American medical aid money to get the little girl into Queen Mary Hospital. "No hope whatsoever," the doctor said. "She's dying of a heart condition."

Despite the loss of her daughter, life eventually became much easier for Mrs. Tsat. Maryknoll staked her to a peddler's license, and put the baby boy into the King's Park nursery where he grew chubby on rice, American surplus powdered milk and a dollar's worth of vitamin pills.

Mrs. Tsat considered herself wealthy again. She had a capital of $1.65 and walked a mile every morning to buy vegetables wholesale, reselling them for a 25-cent daily profit. Her major disappointment was that her husband could not escape from China. Or even write a letter easily. He wrote twice, on the back of a sack, requesting food, but postage is such a luxury in China that he had to go without food for two days to mail each message.

She will probably never see her husband again.

"I never go back to Communism," she said, "and husband not want me to bring baby back to die without food.

American medicine and American people are greatest in world. No question, they the greatest."

The man and his wife could write their names, brush a few Chinese characters, and sometimes understand simple printing. They were typical Chinese refugees. They were the Wong Ban Keung family—a popular name, the American equivalent of which would be John Smith. They received a few dollars' medical help annually.

The Wongs had been young, happy and illiterate, with a patch of land about a hundred miles north of Canton, and had hardly known what the government was until the Communist cadres came in 1951. But they very soon realized that they did not want Communism despite all its promises. They put everything they owned into three grass bags, and with their four children walked to Hong Kong. There was no space in the squatter camps on the Kowloon side, so they crossed the bay to Hong Kong Island, "looking for farmland," and eventually went as far as the geography would allow. Which was Chai Wan and Father Edmond's hillside.

They slept in the streets and under the trees until a Maryknoll lay worker reported the case. The Wongs received free tin and boards for a hut. It was a start and they progressed. Wong raised 85 cents, invested in fresh fish, and peddled it on the streets until he was thrown in jail for not having a license. Father Edmonds convinced headquarters that Wong was honest, and got him off without a fine.

When Wong returned home, he received one of Maryknoll's "letters of introduction." It helped. He was hired for a "glamor" position created by the population rise—a night watchman's job. It paid $17.50 a month. The hours were from the time the factory closed at 6 P.M. until it opened at 7:30 the next morning. He had one day off every month. He had a thirty-minute walk to the bus line; the bus and second-class ferry cost him 10 cents a day—$3 a month, or roughly a sixth of his salary. But Wong loved it.

The children—soon there were five—were very bright. The oldest son received free tuition at a Maryknoll Sisters' school, and the education of the other two would have stopped altogether if their monthly tuition had not been reduced from 52 to 17 cents. They probably would have been able to survive without the American surplus food distributed by Maryknoll, but they might not have lived without the $4 or $5 worth of medicine they received for abscessed teeth, boils, eye infections and chickenpox. It would have been useless to send the little girl to school if the Sister hadn't ordered the family to stop allowing the medicine man to stuff herbs in her infected ears.

Wong held his job because he was able to have an operation for bleeding ulcers which herb magic had not cured. A private hospital would have cost him a year's salary, and he didn't have a week's salary saved; and the waiting list at many more nominal government hospitals is so long that it's almost like winning on the horses every day to get in. Father Edmonds arranged for the operation and allowed Wong to "pay" for it so he wouldn't feel like a beggar. He paid the $3.50 off in three installments. It was a good investment for

Maryknoll. It's cheaper to put a working man back on his feet than it is to feed the whole family.

The Wongs would soon be entirely self-sufficient. The wife took the Maryknoll knitting course and supplemented the family income by 8½ cents a day by making gloves. The money was invested toward getting them back into farming. They bought four chickens which they brought into their 10-by-15-foot house every night and placed under the bed. The younger children carried good dirt up the steep hill for nearly a mile to press against the bottom edges of the hut. They utilized the "extra" space in the house by growing tomato plants in six flowerpots. Wong himself tenderly cared for their fifteen or twenty bean plants.

The Wong Ban Keungs had reached their improvement limit. Their case was not rare. It was representative, and they were one of the luckier families. There were conservatively 200,000 refugees in Hong Kong who would envy such an existence; and of course uncounted millions over the hill in China who would have classified the Wongs as rich.

# 10.

## DAILY BREAD—ONCE A WEEK

**D**ESPITE Maryknoll's refugee work, half of the squatters went to bed without supper.

"We simply scrounged around for handouts," Father Trube admitted, "and when we were lucky, bought food and gave it to the neediest. We got a small stream of contributions from the United States, but it was too small for a regular program. They were from people like the employees of the New York Life Insurance Company and the First National Bank of Yonkers, down to two- and five-dollar contributions from schoolteachers."

Even the "exchange letters" were welcomed: occasionally an American collector offered to send $20 worth of food for a couple of dollars' worth of Hong Kong commemorative postage stamps; another man wanted to add to his salt-and-pepper shaker collection of 4,000 by exchanging food for them.

International organizations were not yet participating, although there were intermittent shipments of United States' surplus foods. But the donations could have a deceptive appearance. Once when 265,000 pounds of surplus milk powder reached Hong Kong and was funneled through parishes to the neediest, a newspaper headlined: THREE AND A HALF MILLION GLASSES OF MILK! But three days later there was no milk.

Famine was so bad that thousands were worse off than one self-supporting widow of seventy. She manufactured a fish net from a discarded window screen and broomstick, opened the top of a sewer, and fished for scraps. She always washed her "catch" on the street in a pail of clear water, then hobbled away, presumably to have her supper alone.

The United States Government was understandably gun shy about donating large shipments. It had attempted distributing relief supplies to the Chinese once before—in China after World War II—and only succeeded in raising the living standard of the black-market gangs. It had learned that foodstuffs cannot be distributed through politicians and amateurs; that even the most humanitarian effort cannot be successful without skilled and dedicated volunteer personnel. So, with the enactment of Public Law 480, Title III, the United States volunteered to distribute surpluses to Hong Kong—but only through local voluntary relief organizations. One of those selected to handle such supplies was Catholic Relief Services,[1] which American bishops

---

[1] The entire distribution of U. S. food in Hong Kong is handled by Church World Service, CARE, Inc., Lutheran World Service, Seventh-Day Adventist Welfare Service and Catholic Relief Services. From 1954–61, agricultural commodities received in Hong Kong totaled $27,258,279.29.

had organized in 1943 for war victims abroad and operated in China until the Communists were in power. Then the operation was transferred from the Catholic Central Bureau of Shanghai to Hong Kong, where Father Paul Duchesne of Maryknoll became its director.

Thus with the help of Catholic Relief Services and United States Government surplus, Maryknoll went to work.

Fathers Duchesne, Trube and Jim Smith, the new Maryknoll superior in Hong Kong, were waiting on Kowloon wharf when the United States' freighter *Edgar Luckenback* nosed in. Its cargo was 275,000 food parcels sent by Americans as Christmas gifts. American bishops had named the worldwide plan "Operation Poinsettia."

This was probably the largest single shipment of food ever to reach Hong Kong. The swinging cranes juggled cases of beans, rice, butter, dried beef, oil, corn meal and eight other kinds of foodstuff. Twenty truckers, working sixteen-hour shifts for three days, were needed to haul the food to one of the principal distribution points—Bishop Ford Center. Additional trucks delivered to 3 other Maryknoll centers and 106 community centers. The shipment was so gigantic that it had a $6,000 local trucking bill.

The Fathers and Sisters had screened the needy at parish level; Father Trube, who not only had to fight off the Walled City's gangs' attempts to steal the food, also had so many needy cases among his 25,000 refugees that he was compelled to give preference to those "who might just starve to death today."

His voice came over the loudspeaker: "Those of you

who have blue tickets, come today. Those with yellow tickets, tomorrow. If your ticket is green, come Thursday. You can come with your red tickets on Friday."

Thirteen and a half pounds of food were put in separate paper shopping bags. No political propaganda was inserted, but each bag had an outside imprint of clasped hands and the inscription: A GIFT FROM THE PEOPLE OF AMERICA.[2]

The first recipient—one of the newer escapees from China —asked where she had to go to listen to the tape recording about the government. Another woman queried: "What do I have to read out loud before I am allowed to receive this?" The gifts, with stark need their only requirement, etched a lasting impression on these desperate people.

It was a festive occasion. The gift parcels had arrived too late for Christmas, but it was the Chinese New Year. A young priest played "dingdong" records over the loud-speaker, and people sang as they moved up in line. (An energetic catechist measured it as two and a half miles long.) Twenty-five thousand refugees were fed over a four-day period in Bishop Ford Center alone. Altogether, over 300,000 refugees[3] benefited from this one shipment.

Maryknoll Sisters were particularly enthusiastic over the powdered milk shipments, which they named "Operation Milky Way." Sister Madelaine Sophie, a Catholic Relief Services distributor, accounted for virtually every glass of milk, and thus contradicted reports of careless distribution.

---

[2] The wording "U.S.A." was simple for the Communists to alter, although their previous attempts to change it to "U.S.S.R." on other donations were so crude that even the Chinese had laughed.

[3] Forty thousand food parcels were sent to refugees in Macao the same day.

(Powdered milk had been used to draw lines for basketball courts in Brazil.)

"Milk was what we really needed," recalled the Sister, "Babies weren't crying normally, but with the peculiar whine of undernourishment and hunger. When we noticed an apparently well-nourished child, a glance at the mother's face told the true story. Her self-sacrifice showed in her hollow cheeks and listless bearing. We tried to give this milk to expectant mothers, the poorest school children, and families we knew to be near starvation."

With the advent of World Refugee Year, shipments and other contributions increased and more refugees were fed. Still, Maryknoll didn't have enough food for all hungry refugees and had to set up an eligibility criterion. Relief supplies were only issued to breadwinners who were unemployed or earned less than $8.75 per week. All cases, whether the needy went to the Catholic Relief Services in the Man Yee Building, or to a local parish, were interviewed to ascertain whether they were eligible.

It was determined that to maintain enough energy to work, a refugee and his wife each required monthly: ½ pound of milk powder, 3 pounds of flour, 3½ pounds of corn meal, 2 pounds of peanut oil, 5 pounds of rice, 4 pounds of crushed wheat and 2 pounds of beans. No one refugee, however, ever received the entire food list in one month. There were never enough supplies to go around.

Maryknoll also branched into a Feed-a-Family program by soliciting Hong Kong $5 bills (87½ cents), buying bags of rice and other essentials, and distributing these to the poorest families and to the most desperate new arrivals.

"Those on steady relief, though," theorized Father Edmonds, "probably wouldn't starve to death if we cut them off. A hungry person is going to steal before he dies. But it keeps many of the children and even older ones from dying slow deaths from malnutrition."

Many refugees virtually "demanded" to know this wonderful person who had donated this food. Many of the literate, and even some of the illiterate, expressed their thanks in letters somewhat like the following:

DEAR FRIEND,

Our original country [China] village is Nancheng. We were business people in Shanghai for more than 10 years. We had a nice home there with a family of eight. After Communist liberation, business went from bad to worse, then nothing at all. So I closed the shop and lived on our savings, but the Reds wanted more than that from us. They accused me of many things that were not true, but I was not allowed to explain. So we left Shanghai for Macao, hoping from here to go to Taiwan where my son teaches in high school. We have waited so long for an entry permit, but it doesn't come. Eight of us are starving. My wife suffered so much she committed suicide last month and left the children to me. We are desperate and hungry.

How can I thank you enough for your wonderful food package through the Sisters at Fatima Mission? Were it not for you we might have died of starvation. You should have seen the eyes of the children when I carried the parcel home. They haven't seen any good food since I forget when. Thank you again.

H.H.W. AND FAMILY

DEAR FRIEND,

Thank you for your help of such a nice food parcel. I don't know how to express my gratitude to you, but we really appreciate your kind help.

We lived in Canton for generations. My father-in-law and his father are returned students from Japan. They are well-educated lawyers, but lawyers are no longer allowed to practice in China. When war broke out against the Japanese, my husband joined the army. He returned after the war and we lived in great peace and unity. We had a good life for three years until the Reds came. First, they accused my grandfather, who was over ninety, of being a landlord, and he died of a heart attack. Then the Communists took my father-in-law and accused him of being a landlord. They killed him. Knowing they would be looking for my husband, who had been a Nationalist soldier, we fled to Hong Kong empty-handed.

We have no relatives now and very few friends here. My husband suffered so much during this time that he got TB. He has lost all interest in living. He sees the children without support, and he can't work because of illness. May God bless you for your generosity and I hope to be able to do the same for others some day.

Gratefully yours,
L.M.Y. AND FAMILY

Father Duchesne had done a superlative job as Catholic Relief Services Director in helping to solve Hong Kong's complex food problem,[4] but now he was needed elsewhere. South Vietnam was alert to the fact that the Viet Cong—Communist infiltrators—were wooing the poor mountain

---

[4] During 1961, a typical year, Catholic Relief Services in Hong Kong received nearly 30 million pounds of foodstuffs from the American agriculture surplus. The value was $1,770,786,86.

peasants there with food promises, and the Maryknoll priest was dispatched there as Catholic Relief Services Director on February 20, 1957.

Maryknoll had a highly capable and effervescent replacement in Monsignor John Romaniello—born in Potenza, Italy, and reared in New Rochelle, New York—who had given the Communists difficulty around Kweilin. A serious and thoroughly dedicated man, Monsignor Romaniello has the added blessing of an invincible spirit of fun. Known as The Jolly Roman, he is a tallish 5 foot 9, of medium build, has a round face on which a smile is thoroughly at home, and is almost bald. Without his collar, he looks a little like a perennially good-natured theatrical comedian. From the poorest squatter's hut to the lobby of the Peninsula Hotel, the grimness of Hong Kong life seemed to lift into a lighter and happier tempo as he appeared.

He was so proficient in both the Cantonese and Mandarin dialects that he could joke with a grandmother about the old country, quote the classics to a scholar, or talk shop with a businessman. And he got to know all of these, and the Chinese got to know him as Loh Man Lo. Another affectionate nickname was Monsignor Moonface.

Like his predecessor, Monsignor Romaniello had one material desire—to feed refugees. But he faced an unexpected and serious problem.

Washington officials had become so aroused by complaints from Hong Kong businessmen that they considered stopping relief shipments. Milling-company executives began calling the American Consulate office in Hong Kong.

An owner would complain that where his company had been selling 50 million pounds of flour annually, the figure was now cut to 30 million. Somebody, the callers complained, was selling United States relief flour on the black market.

When the Monsignor asked for proof, they told him that American flour was being quoted in the daily commodity price lists. Several millers cabled the United States Department of Agriculture, and Washington wired its Hong Kong office to investigate.

While the United States Department of Agriculture was indeed generous, the food was appropriately named—surplus. The thing was that flour and corn meal were surplus to the Chinese too. Although they had fled from a country that had specialized in gastronomy—everything from snake and dog meat simmered in rice wine to the renowned Peking duck—they could not use flour and corn meal.

South China's basic diet has always been rice—the easiest food to digest. Corn meal is one of the hardest. Despite the refugees' hunger, they simply could not digest corn meal. As for the flour—how could they cook it? In most refugee huts the only cooking utensil was a single pot. There wasn't an oven in the entire refugee area. Hungry refugees took the only road out—they sold the flour and corn meal to hawkers for 5 Hong Kong cents a pound, and the hawkers resold it to bakers in hundred-pound lots. And even some of the Catholic distributors had been trying to circumvent the black-market operators by sending the flour to bakeries to be made into bread for refugees.

Twenty percent of the flour was used as the bakers' payment. The refugee was being shorted.

Monsignor Romaniello trailed one nine-year-old girl as she left a flour line. She automatically carried the five-pound bag to a bakery and exchanged it for a smaller portion of rice noodles. She didn't mind being cheated.

The Monsignor did not have the immediate answer, but he knew that this American act of generosity was breaking the law. United States Public Law No. 480 specifies that no relief supplies are to be distributed if they upset the economic status of an area. If this law is violated, all relief will be discontinued.

"And," the monsignor said, "we were doing exactly that —breaking the law."

# 11.

## NOODLES IN THE MORNING

MONSIGNOR Romaniello investigated further and checked with two hundred bakers; they testified that the little girl's swap for noodles was not an isolated case. Almost every baker had traded noodles or bread for government flour or corn meal.

The situation worried the priest. What if the food we had wasn't fit to eat? he asked himself. Same thing with the refugees. Here these starving people don't know where their next meal is coming from, and we give them five-pound bags of food they can't eat.

"The logical solution," Monsignor Romaniello contended, "would be to give the refugees bread instead of flour." But neither Maryknoll nor the Catholic Relief Services had the facilities for large ovens. What few they had were scrapped from American ships.

One day, walking through the granite buildings of Maryknoll's Ngau Tau Kok Center, the monsignor found the answer. A Chinese helper was mixing dough in a tub, then pushing it into the hopper of a hand-cranked machine. The dough came out in a thin sheet and was cut into strips and dried on a clothesline.

Monsignor Moonface beamed as he thought, This man is making noodles. Just like that little girl wanted.

"Now look, how many pounds of that stuff can you make in a day?" he questioned.

"If it's sunny weather," the man answered in Cantonese dialect, "about forty pounds."

Off the monsignor went to corner Father McKiernan and suggest that Maryknoll go into the noodle business.

"No, I'm not crazy." He laughed. "This may be the answer."

He studied the dough presser, which resembled a washing-machine wringer, and did some calculating. Then he drove over to San Shue Po, a heavily congested district occupied by former ironworkers from Shanghai. He explained what he wanted, showed them a crude drawing he called a blueprint, and asked the price.

"It'll be six hundred Hong Kong dollars [$105] for the one machine," the foundry man said, "and two hundred dollars [$35] for a motor. Going to make noodles, you say, with this machine? Look, Father—we guarantee the machine will operate, but we don't guarantee that it will make noodles."

"Then just make one," the priest replied, "and we'll see how it works."

Father McKiernan said he knew a "secret laboratory." It was the stained clapboard garage at Bishop Ford Center. Father Trube backed his car out of the garage, and it became a noodle laboratory. The noodle-making contraption was hauled in one August morning. That night a typhoon ripped the roof off the garage. After repairing it, Monsignor Romaniello worked on his formula. He began with corn meal and used a Chinese assistant's family as guinea pigs. The family broke out in a burning rash; rice-eating Chinese could not make the sudden adjustment to hard-to-digest corn meal.

"Look, you're no mean amateur chef yourself," the monsignor told Father Trube. "Get your recipe book. Say, why don't we use some of that powdered milk and flour? Think of all the calories in that!"

They mixed a paste in a washtub, fed it through the machine, dried the yard-long noodles and broke them into 12-inch lengths. Then they boiled them with a couple of pieces of bacon for flavor.

Another guinea pig was picked. Monsignor Romaniello watched while the man ate without expression, then solemnly held out his bowl for more.

"Fellows," the monsignor quipped, "we're in the noodle business."

The hand-cranked machine could produce fifty pounds

of noodles daily. They had just enough money for ten more machines. The monsignor returned to the foundry, but the men there had thrown away his "blueprint" and he had to begin all over.

With eleven machines turning out noodles and making a few refugees happier, the monsignor took a side trip to Japan. He discovered something that downgraded his status as an inventor, but settled much of the food problem. Tokyo had thousands of electrically operated noodle machines that required only two operators instead of the five that Romaniello's hand-cranked job did. Moreover, they were considerably cheaper.

So the Jolly Roman convinced both the Hong Kong government and American representatives that noodles could solve everything. The United States Government donated $40,000 for the purchase of huge noodle machines to be used by volunteer relief organizations.

Within a year Monsignor Romaniello had twenty-five factories working sixteen-hour shifts and producing ½ million pounds of noodles a month. Seven machines were installed in the Portuguese colony of Macao. They spread like an infection—to Vietnam, Tibet, Burma, Laos, Taiwan, Ethiopia, the Philippines, Peru, Liberia and Bolivia.

The popularity was universal. Noodles were ready to cook. They could be boiled alone, or mixed with bean sprouts, liver or broth.

The most typifying testimonial came from a sweaty coolie who approached Monsignor Romaniello in a warehouse one day.

"Father," he began bashfully, "I want to thank you for your noodles. They have changed our whole life."

"Yeah."

"But, Father," he continued, "don't get me wrong. I don't take handouts every day. I live with my family on a rooftop and get up very early looking for work. Sometimes I am lucky and find a day's work and make four or five dollars [85 cents]. But many days I do not find work, and go home resentful. I say to myself, Maybe I was not sharp enough today. I really go home ashamed.

"See, we leave Communists for Hong Kong because they not only starve us, but tell us when to blow our noses and when to cross our legs. Here, it is free and I want to work, but I cannot. Many nights we do not eat. I was so ashamed. Now, when I come home and have to tell the wife that I was not able to find work, she pulls out some noodles, puts them in our pot, and we all eat like everything is normal."

The Hong Kong *Tiger Standard* headlined a story about noodles: THE BEST THING IN TOWN—TASTY NOODLES MADE OUT OF U. S.-DONATED FLOUR FEED REFUGEES.

The monsignor's noodles not only sidelined some black marketeers and revolutionized the distribution of surplus foods, but also transformed the priest into Hong Kong's most colorful celebrity. Hollywood seeks movie rights to his "noodle life story."

"All my spiritual work, my thousands of masses and all my teaching"—Monsignor Romaniello theorizes—"nobody remembers me for them. I've received more attention from noodles."

Moreover, the noodle popularity transformed the persuasive monsignor into an extroverted crusader for noodles. After the first machine began to roll them out, he started a letter campaign soliciting additional machines. No one of any significance visited Hong Kong without inspecting the noodle factories, giving noodles to refugees, and of course giving a donation. During one six-month stretch his noodle handlers included Royal Dutch Airline hostesses, broadcasters Huntley and Brinkley, schoolteachers, singers, bankers, doctors, students, jockey Eddie Arcaro and professional golfers Gene Sarazen and Peter Thomson.

Attorney General Robert Kennedy toured Southeast Asia in 1962, and Monsignor Romaniello persuaded him to visit Bishop Ford Center. Just as Bobby Kennedy reached the hilltop parish his host exploded 200 firecrackers.

The startled Attorney General poked his fingers in his ears, laughed, and asked, "What's all that for?"

"Because we're all Chinese here," Monsignor Romaniello replied.

The Attorney General spent fifteen minutes handing out five-pound bags of noodles.

The Romaniello sense of humor is irresistible. Most Hong Kong places are prefaced by the word "royal"—such as the Royal Hong Kong Country Club or Royal Hong Kong Hospital—and the monsignor strolls into the British clubs with a yellow leather bag, simply engraved NOODLES, and snaps, "Royal Noodle Company, Limited, sir." The bag was a gift from the golfers at Happy Valley golf course.

"Noodles" Romaniello is the most consistent winner on the par 72 course. A high 70's golfer, he baits people into playing him for "One hundred dollars a game," Hong Kong money, of course ($17.50), and his winnings go to noodles. He seldom loses, but when he does he remarks, "Now aren't you ashamed of yourself—taking noodles away from children?" He also delights in writing "Noodle Business" in the occupation columns of registration forms he has to fill out.

Although Monsignor Romaniello usually spends a nine-to-five day in the office of Catholic Relief Services, he also spends considerable off-duty time in the Peninsula Hotel's popular tearoom lobby. Soliciting for noodles, of course. He was there for this interview and was highly enthusiastic.

"Good news!" he exulted. "Money'll be rolling in for the refugee now. When Huntley and Brinkley came through, I told them it was their duty to plug noodles. Just got word that they had some little Chinese kids sing the noodle song on their TV program."

He agreed to dinner in the Marco Polo Room in the connecting Peninsula Court. "See all these paintings of Marco Polo," he said as we walked down the carpeted steps. "Those are Marco Polo and noodles. See, Marco was an Italian who came to China and brought the noodle to Italy. I'm an Italian missioner. I'm bringing it back."

A man in the corner waved, and Monsignor Romaniello asked how he was feeling. "Real good," the American said. "Down from a hundred and eighty-five to a hundred and seventy-two pounds and never touched Metrecal."

"That proves it," Romaniello quipped. "Caught you red-handed. You've been eating the noodles that belong to the refugee."

He scanned the 24-by-30-inch printed menu that is a collector's item, then called for the waiter. "It's not on the menu, but we'd like something with noodles in it."

The headwaiter and the chef finally produced veal cutlet with noodles instead of spaghetti. "It makes me ashamed to eat this." The monsignor frowned. "Here we have such a selection and there are a billion people who will go to bed without any supper at all tonight. Lot of refugees in Hong Kong didn't eat, and that's why I don't mind crusading for noodles. Anyway, there are a hundred and thirty-five local agencies looking for help in Hong Kong and we have to go outside for contributions. How's your noodles? You know, the refugee noodles are much better than these. See, these are made with water, and we use powdered milk for more nutrition. Our noodles are too expensive for even the expensive places like this to cook.

"Here's a good example. A refugee lady stopped me on the street and asked, 'Why are these noodles better than before?'

"I told her that we were using milk powder now.

"'I thought there was something new,' she told me. 'They're the best noodles I've ever eaten. They've even got an ice-cream taste.'

"I asked her how in the world she knew what ice cream tasted like. She had never had any.

"The old lady grinned sheepishly and said, 'Once we had

132

some money and bought an ice-cream stick for the children. And I just took a little bite to see what it tasted like.'

"These Chinese are very self-sacrificing. They'll always take care of the children first.

"And these noodles have helped clear up their skins. Before they ate noodles—we put in vitamins too—they had all kinds of skin disorders.

"Let me add this. My boyhood friend, Anthony Tyrone, the founder of Hamilton Mutual Funds in Denver, is an oilman and is also connected with a movie studio. Wants to make a movie out of the refugees and noodles—he was so impressed with the dignity and determination of the refugees in such surroundings. 'They eat their rice and noodles,' he said, 'on the side of the road or street, as proud as a man in a castle.' Anthony's done a lot for noodles."

Eddie Guzman, the band leader, interrupted. Monsignor Romaniello exchanged greetings and requested the "special song" for the American visitor. The band began a rendition of something to the tune of "Sugar in the Morning." Then Eddie sang:

> Noodles in the morning
> Noodles in the evening
> Noodles at suppertime
> Be my daily noodles and
> Feed me all the time.
>
> Boil them in the morning
> Fry them in the evening
> Cook them anytime.
> Just try Romy's noodles
> You'll choose them every time.

The crowd applauded.

"You should have been here the first time," the priest whispered. "I was with some people who had money and they should have donated more to noodles. I got them to sing the noodle song at the table—right here—and they dared me to get up and sing it myself. So I thought, why should I be ashamed of doing anything to feed hungry people? I got up and sang the noodle song. Before I left, we'd raised four thousand Hong Kong dollars [$700] for noodles."

The bubbly monsignor has indeed become the "Noodle King." He received a postcard from Rome addressed only to "The Noodle King of Hong Kong." Word spread to Los Angeles, where some children held a neighborhood benefit show and mailed $8 to "Noodles, Hong Kong." Walter O'Malley, President of the Los Angeles Dodgers, made a sizable contribution, and it was matched by Hollywood personalities like Bob Cummings and Art Linkletter.

One day Monsignor Romaniello's secretary received a call saying that someone from Hollywood wanted to hand out noodles.

"I didn't recall the name—Laura LaPlante—at first," the priest said. "Then we got to talking and I mentioned that I grew up in New Rochelle, New York. 'That's where I made one of my first pictures,' Miss LaPlante said."

The noodle campaigner didn't let the fact that Miss La-Plante had been a heroine of silent movie serials escape notice. He informed the local Hong Kong movie industry that people had traveled from Hollywood to help noodles, and persuaded Run Run Shaw, the M.G.M. of Hong Kong, to sponsor a noodle fund-raising première for the movie *Back Door*, a story of family life that won the best-film award at the Asia Film festival. The priest brought along a photographer, announced that a family that eats together stays together, and photographed the cast holding paper bags of noodles. They raised almost $3,000.

A few days later Monsignor Romaniello got a telephone call from a Mr. Bryan of Los Angeles. "I'm over at the Astor Hotel in Kowloon," he explained, "and I've been hearing a lot about noodles back in L.A."

"I'll be right over," the missioner said, "as soon as I can get a ferry."

The priest explained the program, but Mr. Bryan never gave a dime. "When I get home," he explained, "I'll get something going for noodles."

Romaniello brushed it off as a dry run. A couple of months later he received a cablegram from Los Angeles:

MITE BOX RAN THIRD. YOUR SHARE IN MAIL. MITE BOX
NEEDS HELP RUNNING TOMORROW SANTA ANITA.

J. C. BRYAN

"Well, the only thing to do," Monsignor Romaniello said, "was roll my eyes heavenward." Needless to say, Mite Box won by two lengths. Three days later the priest received the air-mail letter and check. And Mite Box, an aptly named two-year-old son of Moolah Box, was running for noodles. Ten percent of his earnings was sent to the monsignor's fund. The father called him the Noodle Mascot and used the $1,000 for his twenty-sixth noodle unit. It's named Mite Box Noodle Factory.

Noodle unit No. 27 acquired the yacht name, The Nassau Special. Monsignor Romaniello had discovered a tourist who was a writer for the Nassau *Daily Tribune* in the Bahamas, and had promptly brainwashed him. The man opened a sales pitch for noodle donations by producing the following editorial in the August 21, 1961 issue:

> One day a rich man opened his eyes and found himself in a hell of a spot. In fact, he was in hell. And as he cast his eyes toward heaven he saw Lazarus there, and he cried to him for help. In that moment he would have paid all the wealth he had on earth for just one little drop of water to cool his parched tongue.
>
> We can all think of moments in our lives when a drink of water—or some other small thing—was of paramount importance. Nineteen years ago in the bush at Mayaguana, a man who was then a stranger to us gave us a cup of coffee and provided us with a bath. We have since become close friends and we have lost no opportunity to help him. He doesn't understand when we still thank him for that cup of coffee. He cannot understand that, at that particular moment, if we had to choose between a gold mine and a cup of coffee, the coffee would have won.
>
> If we asked you in this column today, how important is a NOODLE to you, you may think we are being ridiculous. But in Hong Kong . . .

Monsignor Romaniello regards Communist China as an ulcer. "And somebody has to cut it out," he tells you. "Look, how can we ever have peaceful coexistence with Communism? They have no value on life. In the U.S. we give a man a trial even if he confesses to murder. We still have to prove

136

it before we sentence a human. When I was in Red China, one official told me that nothing matters but the state. 'You Americans think nothing of chopping down a virgin forest to make room for more people,' the man said. 'If we liquidate a hundred million people for the same reason, what of it? People are no different than trees.' "

Another night at dinner, in the Ambassador Hotel, the priest frowned at an American couple leaving half of a steak. "Sure is a pity," he said. "Look at that. We're guilty too, spending more for dinner than some people will have in a year. Food and the art of giving could very well decide World War Three."

He makes his point clear: "We spend ninety billion in foreign aid and it makes the people hate us. Why? We make people feel like beggars. Here's the United States' attitude— 'I'm rich and have a lot of shoes; in fact, I have more shoes than anybody in the world. But I don't like some of them.' So we go to a poor man and say, 'I don't like these shoes and since you look sloppy and appear to be needing shoes, I'm going to give you some of my extra shoes. You know, a handout.'

"We should be telling these people, 'Look, I'm your friend and I'd like you to have these shoes.' We need to light a fire to the imagination of the people in Washington. You can't go to a hut where people are starving and say, 'Here's a bag of flour. Now bake yourself a cake.' You don't do that when you give gifts. You don't give to beggars or people you dislike. You give to your friends, and you wrap, decorate and present your gift in a pleasing manner. You also write a note and say you hope they like it. Give with dignity, not, 'Here's something for you because we don't want it.' Everyone likes to give. During the Middle Kingdom of China, people would travel for weeks to present gifts to the emperor. They were proud to give, even though he would give them a gift a thousand times better.

"If we had given food in a correct manner, we wouldn't have the serious Communist problem in China today. But we've always had a wrong idea. After World War Two, there were two things needed. Europe lacked raw materials to rebuild after the heavy bombings. They got them through the Marshall Plan. Asia, or China, needed food. You couldn't give them the same things people in Europe needed; they didn't know what to do with them. You must give the right thing.

"A billion people won't have a meal tonight. Any night. So they can't have much imagination or drive when they get up. I've seen the people in China. They hated to see Communism come, and knew it was bad. But some of them went Communist because of our attitude: 'China isn't worth the powder used to blow it up.' The people were hungry, and when the Reds promised them something—even though they didn't get it—the hungry masses went along. I've been with the refugees all over Southeast Asia and the Communists have absolutely no standing anywhere. Yet Communism is creeping up in these places. Why? No one in the world wants to go hungry. The only place Communism is making headway is in hungry places. Which goes back to the theory that we should feed hungry people in Asia as our friends and not as beggars. That would further discredit Communism. I've seen it work. Even with a sack of noodles.

"Every day I hand out noodles to the poor who have registered and have a ticket. Sometimes they just go coldly through the line. An old Chinese lady gave me her ticket the other day, and I paused slightly before handing her a two-pound sack of noodles. She gave me the stare.

" 'Look, I gave you my ticket, now where's my noodles?' A boy helping me said, 'He's your friend, why don't you say thanks?' Her face brightened and she said, 'Thank you.' Every time she's in line she can't wait to say Thank you. I even hear her in line, saying 'Our American friends are really nice.' The other day she wanted to give me a gift— an orange.

"I've been working with people who accept Communism and those who reject it, and I know that boy isn't going to accept it. He will fight it and he will help our American friends. That boy is so enthusiastically anti-Communist he wants to go with any landing party that attacks Communist China.

"The United States has spent more than two billion on foreign aid in Laos. Yet we were chased out of the country, and many of the people won't fight. Why? People are starving. Our 'experts' went in and assessed the situation. They decided to build the people a nice road, dam and hotel. Yet people starved. Without food, humans simply cannot develop wealth, or function, or care who runs the government. In the three places where Communism is gaining the fastest—Asia, Africa and South America—people are only four hundred calories a day short of starvation. Most people die before their fortieth birthdays. Unless we feed them and give them a start, they will always be poor. Political instability comes from hunger. Here's my plan to help correct the situation: the U.S. has the funds in the agency for international development and two billion dollars in foreign aid; it has an abundance in agriculture—the Food For Peace Program; it has the Peace Corps, which gives instruction. I suggest we coordinate branches of these three organizations into a food unit that would be available for starving countries. One has the money, one has the agriculture to put these people on a sound footing, and the third has the knowledge.

"Starving or hungry people don't have the time, energy or inclination to fight off Communism. But if they are Christians and aren't hungry, Communism has absolutely no place to gain a major foothold. It doesn't have any with the people who are receiving noodles."

# 12.

## HONG KONG GOES TO SCHOOL

**M**ANY refugees still went hungry—for education. Half of Hong Kong's population was under fifteen years old, and had such a craving for education that there was a demand for "wildcat schools." Some men claiming to be educated taught children in shacks or out under the trees for little more than meals. The government officially disapproved, but was compelled to wink at them. Even Communist schools were crowded.

Primary schools had been Maryknoll's bargaining point in obtaining Crown land for the four refugee areas. Maryknoll did not have the funds to build large schools, but it had the generous backing of the Hong Kong Education Department, which—like every segment of the colony's government—admitted it was overwhelmed by refugees. In addition to the land, the government contributed 50 percent of Maryknoll's school construction expense, lent 30 percent interest free, and paid for all equipment, maintenance and teachers' salaries. Maryknoll was to administer the schools, with the government's single stipulation being the periodic inspection it made of all colony schools.

All four schools were to be on the elementary level. Abruptly, however, the education department informed Maryknoll that its Kowloonstai School must also include a secondary, or high-school level. The department proposed that Father Peter Rielly, who became Maryknoll's education supervisor, head the school.

The switch was to counter the Communists. They had sneaked the only secondary school into Kowloonstai, just forty-five yards up the hill from the Maryknoll school. While the Hong Kong government does not lease land to Communists for schools, it does not interfere with any schools already operating. So a Communist-front man constructed an "apartment house," then converted it into the Nine Little Dragons School.

The maneuver followed the Communist's technique of poisoning children's brains as they grow. "Give me the child," Lenin said, "and I will own the man."

The Maryknoll Fathers' Kowloonstai school—a twenty-four-room stone building, was sliced into morning and afternoon sessions, thereby allowing an enrollment of 1,080. There was an overwhelming number of applications of all denominations for the opening class in 1956, although qualified Catholics received preference.

The best way to judge a school is, of course, from the inside, but it was not simple for strangers to visit the inside of this school. You had to find an enterprising cab driver willing to weave through the teeming streets, swerving around peddlers, carts and stands. Finally you got out and walked up to the wire fence that refugees utilized as a community clothesline.

There was a contrasting orderliness inside the two school buildings, which are connected by a porch. A typical class was secondary-level Form 5 Literature, which had a 100 percent attendance.[1] All 24 boys and 10 girls, neatly dressed in blue and white, were seated well before the 8:30 A.M. bell rang. Instructor Gerald Kent read aloud as almost every student traced each word of the book, *The Lost World*. He stopped often to define difficult words, and selected volunteers for oral reading. Nearly every hand went up. There was no casual listening or faking.

It was hot, sticky Hong Kong weather, and the second-story window was raised. It not only let in air, but also a continuous shrill chant of hawkers, crashing sounds resembling truckloads of tin cans being emptied, screams like those in a good horror movie, and the crescendos of family arguments in advanced stages. The only break came from the roar of jets' exhausts blasting the school's roof as they approached nearby Kai Tak Airport runway stretching a mile and a half into Kowloon Bay. During the entire class not one student ever looked toward the window or seemed aware of any disturbance.

[1] The average is 98.9 percent for the entire school.

143

"The students' application is routine," said the bespectacled Father Rielly, who passed by in the hallway from
his English class, one of the sixteen courses he teaches a
week. "You bet they bear down," he said. "Even if a student enrolled in the English section passes or makes good
grades in everything else, he must pass English or repeat
the entire year. You have to speak English to be employed
in Hong Kong, and that's why we run the school in two
sections—English and Chinese—with English being taught
as a foreign subject in the Chinese section.[2] We contend
that both English and Chinese should be taught, not only
for balance but because Chinese is pretty important to
Chinese people."

Father Rielly led the way to his office, where we discussed
Maryknoll's schools. "See all those ragged and dirty little kids outside," he began, "kids who people thought
couldn't learn anything. We've only graduated two high-
school classes, but those same dirty little kids are now on
academic scholarships in places like Notre Dame, the University of Illinois, Ohio State, and the University of Mel-
bourne. Here, look at the record books."

The books revealed that Maryknoll's Kowloonstai primary school sponsored an average of seventy-four students
in taking the colony's compulsory examination for high-
school entrance. And while the average for promotion was
only 25 percent in Hong Kong, Maryknoll students scored

---

[2] Maryknoll's first Cantonese-English textbooks were written by Father
Frederick Dietz and later fully developed by Father Thomas O'Melia; Father
Bernard Meyer compiled the Cantonese-English dictionary.

a percentage of 65. Three students had won five-year scholarships.

All the students are extremely poor, pointed out Mrs. S. Y. Tong, the Edinburgh graduate who served as the school's headmistress. "And most of them had never been associated with English-speaking people before they came here. But they work hard to overcome the handicap. Most of them have no lights to study by at home."

There are many students who have found school openings through the generosity of Americans. Such as the thin boy of about fifteen who walked into Father Rielly's office and received a $10 Hong Kong bill ($1.75).

"Kid's named Robert Lee," Father Rielly explained. "In April of sixty-one, a man named Carl Romer called the American Consulate here and inquired about where he could send a poor student through school. They told him to call Maryknoll, so I got in touch with him."

The caller, a landscape contractor from Santa Monica, California, explained his proposal. When a boy, Romer himself had been spotted by a rich oilman whose hobby was making education possible for poor kids. Now Romer was doing the same thing. He had sent thirty-six students through school, and many had become lawyers and doctors.

"I've been all over the world," Romer told Father Rielly, "and I've never met a more polite kid than the one carrying bags today at the Ambassador Hotel. Very willing worker. Only fourteen, and supporting his mother and two sisters on a hundred and fifty Hong Kong dollars a month. What's that? A little over twenty-five dollars in American money? I'd like to send him through school. I'll give him his hotel salary as an allowance."

Father Rielly took both names, and next afternoon went to the Ambassador, located the boy, and discussed Romer's offer with him in Chinese, although the boy had learned a little English from tourists.

The priest thought Robert Lee had the "proper attitude." The boy was extremely grateful, and the hotel was pleased that he had the opportunity. Father Rielly found him an extra seat in Form 2, and Robert Lee became a B student.

"Now see that little girl over there," Father Rielly continued. "Catherine Chan. Eight years old and one of our best third-grade students. Another generous American is responsible."

During the 1960 tourist season, Byron Picton of San Francisco told his cab driver to point out places of interest around Hong Kong. There really wasn't much to see in the section they were in, and the driver showed him mostly schools.

"Which one of these schools do your kids go to?" Picton asked.

"That's what really hurts me," the driver, Paul Chan, said. "I can't get my little girls in school. All schools are filled except the very expensive private ones, and that's way too much money for me."

Picton took the driver's name and address, and wrote Maryknoll Bishop John W. Comber in New York about sponsoring the children. An investigation showed that Paul Chan's mother had been educated in Idaho, had become a teacher and had married a University of Canton professor.

His father had died from Communist mistreatment before the family could escape. All of the cab driver's children became A students.

Another time, a coolie, Yip Chor Hing, who had been given a servant's job at the school by Father Rielly, mentioned that his little girls were "just as smart as these around here." He wasn't mistaken. Father Rielly found someone to pay their expenses and got them into the school. They didn't need a sponsor long. The oldest girl was among the 7,000 candidates for ninety government scholarships. She won one.

The 12:45 P.M. bell rang, ending the school's first shift and giving the staff an hour's break before the second group arrived. As the children walked to the street they intermingled with first-shift students from the Nine Little Dragons School. The kids were the same age and dressed much alike, but there was a contrast. The Communist students stared coldly and suspiciously at those from Maryknoll.

This is only natural. The Nine Little Dragons School doesn't completely emphasize such subjects as civics, geology, Chinese history and literature, English and Biblical knowledge. There they read aloud from China mainland magazines and newspapers and discuss stories such as the United States' problems in Little Rock and at the University of Mississippi, and "warmongering in Korea and Vietnam."

Nine Little Dragons and other Communist schools avoid attention. There is very little outside activity, except for lookout youngsters posted in their schoolyards on the watch for government inspectors. Hong Kong schools are not allowed to become "political."

No Maryknoll school has ever lost a student to a Communist school, and their personnels have little difficulty spotting Communist "ringers" trying to recruit among their student bodies. "The students will tip off the teachers when there might be a Commie present," Father Rielly contended, "but we usually screen them out before they get in. The second year here we had a bunch of applications from Communist kids—pictures and all. But it worked out smoothly. They had such bad backgrounds—no English at all—that they would have failed their classes anyway."

"Communist schools have one advantage over ours." Father Rielly laughed. "Certainly more extracurricular activities. They teach the children to distribute pamphlets secretly; or they'll have them invite six or seven other kids to their homes for tea. They're usually sons of merchants dealing with Communists and can afford it. They feed them, all right. Anti-West propaganda. And with the ridiculous lies and hatred against the West those people up on the hill are teaching, I feel it is my responsibility to tell my students the truth about the horrible conditions on the mainland—tell them what I actually saw and experienced there."

There was a Communist school—actually a shack with a Communist flag on it—about a hundred yards from Bishop Ford Center until it was transferred to a fourth-floor flat in the Walled City.

"They educate—if that's what you call propaganda," noted Father Trube, "the kids of families in unions and those doing business with the Commies. But they want all the non-Communist children they can get. They prefer older ones who can be influenced to do a Communist job. The families around here don't have to tell their children to keep away from Commie kids because they're bad and all that. They keep at a distance anyway after any contact with them. Commie kids are no fun to play with. Ten-year-olds don't like or can't really understand talk about imperialists and capitalists and war and spying all the time. And that's all the Communist kids know.

"Occasionally the poor, who've sent their children to Communist schools in the belief that they would lose their jobs if they didn't, have a change of heart and ask to transfer them to our schools. We check into them, and if they're honest, we accept them on trial. Ninety-nine percent of them forget all about the Communist propaganda within a week, and the smartest ones don't even need that long."

While Maryknoll Sisters have operated a school in Hong Kong for a long time and have branched into refugee primary schools with the Fathers, they also expanded into a different type of schooling. They began the "Poor School" on the ground floor of the convent, but formally called it the "Boys-Girls Club" to minimize embarrassment. The 114 Poor School students are in three two-hour sessions of studying (reading, writing and arithmetic only), handwork (making plastic flowers and sewing) and civic responsibility.

Children may attend for six years, but one frail little girl who never graduated remains as most endearing in the minds of Sisters Maria Crucia and Marie Thomas. Her name was

Au Siu Mooi (Little Peach Blossom), and she first caught Sister Thomas' eye during a Sunday visit at the Shek Kip Mei Resettlement area. Peach Blossom, then eight years old, was particularly cute, with her old China haircut, but her small, careworn face was touching.

She deliberately persisted at her cooking when Sister Thomas bent over to speak to her in Cantonese. After the ice was broken, Siu Mooi said that she had never been inside a school, but that it didn't really matter; she could not afford the time. She had enough problems trying to cook an ample rice-and-greens meal on 5½ cents a day for her four-year-old brother and six-year-old sister.

Peach Blossom's mother had been a schoolteacher and the daughter of a wealthy family in China. But she had such difficulty adjusting to poverty and finding employment in Hong Kong, that she couldn't bear it any longer and abandoned her children. Peach Blossom's father worked as a dock coolie, but was only paid while the company's ships were unloading. Although he was required to be on call twelve hours a day, he actually never worked or was paid for more than 7 or 8 days a month. But if he missed a day seeking another job, he would lose this one.

The case was presented to Sister Rose Victor, Maryknoll's Sister Superior in Hong Kong, and she arranged for delicate little Siu Mooi to attend the Poor School, and put the two younger children in the King's Park nursery. Siu Mooi specialized in sewing and worked on projects at home until midnight for a few extra pennies.

Students like Peach Blossom usually are undernourished,

and all are given vitamins, milk and bread. The Sisters noticed that Peach Blossom never ate much, and if she thought no one was looking, hid her vitamins. She was saving them for her brother Sai Lo.

One day she came to school with her jaws badly swollen. Sister Maria Fidelis, the doctor, examined her and gave her a penicillin shot to combat the infection caused by teeth rotting past the gums. When she later appeared too ill to eat, Sister Thomas took her home in a taxi. Before they reached the resettlement area, Peach Blossom grew worse, and the Sister told the driver to make a U-turn and stop instead at the Kowloon Government Hospital. Besides the infection, the doctors diagnosed her condition as acute leukemia. The Sisters brought food and cookies to her at the hospital, but whenever they turned their heads, Siu Mooi hid the food for her little brother. He never got the cookies. She died five days later.

A case history with a happier ending stands out in the mind of Sister Mary de Ricci, Supervisor of the Maryknoll Convent Secondary School that numbers 741 students. It had helped a farmer from Canton get a job as gardener at St. Teresa Hospital, and enrolled his young daughter in the sixth year of primary school. The girl led her class and excelled during five years of secondary school. When graduation drew near, she and her classmates were talking about the future.

"I'll be going to college in America," the girl said.

"College in America?" questioned Sister Mary de Ricca.

"That would be wonderful, of course, but where in the world are you going to get that kind of money?"

"I haven't eaten one lunch in my six years here." She grinned. "And I saved the money. It will get me to the West Coast."

They got a report on her recently. "One of the top students in the junior class at Seattle University."

But education in Hong Kong is an almost insurmountable problem. A new government-built school opens—on the average—every ten days, and still they cannot catch up with the exploding population. Moreover, there is no room for additional schools unless some new land is contrived. And Maryknoll is doing exactly that.

When a seven-year-old girl fell and nearly died for lack of medical facilities in the Kun Tong section, Father Mc-Kiernan received permission to enter the area with a dispensary. Then as land was reclaimed from the sea and a new community sprang up Maryknoll added its St. John the Baptist School, with Father Edward L. Krumplemann, a husky, sandy-haired priest, to help on the project and to join Fathers John D. Moore and John E. Gatner in teaching two sessions daily.

Meanwhile, Father Jim Smith, former Maryknoll supervisor in Hong Kong, opened another school in 1962. The land? Bordering a cemetery near Bishop Ford Center there was a rocky plot that was inadequate for graves.

# 13.

## MANY HEADS–MANY HEARTS

**H**ONG KONG is not only indescribably poor, but also indescribably generous. Maryknoll is but one example of volunteer work. Actually the main Catholic work is done by the Milan Fathers, who have charge of the diocese, and Maryknollers are engaged in just a portion of refugee areas.

Since the true meaning of charity is not who gives how much and when, Maryknoll should not be ranked. Perhaps Father McKiernan best assessed Hong Kong's situation over coffee at the Peak Café as he studied its panoramic view of the city.

"It's taken a near miracle to remedy the situation out there." He pointed. "But there's been accomplishment on top of accomplishment. The oldest rivalries are those

153

between religious orders, but everybody—people who've been in the field for thirty or forty years—unanimously agrees that Hong Kong is the only place where all religious orders are working together happily. You don't hear of bickering. There's just too much to do. This has been like a big bucket, and Maryknoll's contribution has been one drop. There have been plenty of drops from others. And the government has poured in help. The outsider would think the situation would be pretty well in hand. But it can't be when there's a bottomless bucket. No one organization can do enough." [1]

But they're all trying, and it is as difficult to credit the work of all volunteers in Hong Kong as it would be to take an accurate census, which the government confesses is impossible.

The Hong Kong government, once it realized that refugees were permanent residents, unquestionably has been the leader in assistance; it now donates 30 percent of its budget to refugee aid. Next comes the Hong Kong Council of Social Services, which coordinates the work of ninety-six volunteer agencies. And the largest individual contributors are the American religious organizations—which draw heavily as distributors of U. S. surplus foods—such as the Catholic Relief Services, Church World Service and Lutheran World Service.

[1] Kenneth Kenn, who has had thirty years' experience in various Hong Kong government departments, including that of social welfare director during some of Hong Kong's most critical years, said that he knew of no finer example of cooperation in the world than that which existed between government and private relief agencies there.

Nearly everyone who lives in Hong Kong has a pet charity, and this results in a broad variety of contributors. Such as the woman named Kwong Yeung-yau, who set a Hong Kong and possibly a world's record on March 27, 1962, by giving refugees 1,100 injections from her mobile van in three hours—an average of 5 ½ shots a minute. Or the group called the "Street Sleepers' Shelter Society," which searches the streets for clients every evening. It houses 180 nightly at three shelters—a playground converted into what it describes as "a cosy dormitory" by the erection of canvas screens and bunks, a shelter on Hospital Road and a hut.

Young American men have assisted wholeheartedly, from a group called the Yale Bachelors, which teaches at New Asia College and spends two nights a week working with refugees, to U.S. sailors. Father Cyril V. Hirst, a Maryknoll priest who directs the portside servicemen's stations, discredits the time-honored theory that sailors run directly from ships for Hong Kong's alley saloons. He has seen so many U.S. sailors contribute that he classifies them as "walking goodwill."

Vice-Admiral William Schoech, Commander of the U.S. Seventh Fleet, discussed his men's behavior and charity in Hong Kong aboard the nuclear-powered flagship USS *Oklahoma City*. He had sufficient reason to be proud. In 1961, the U.S. Seventh Fleet—which uses Hong Kong only for a rest stop—was the second largest blood donor to the Hong Kong Red Cross. It gave 1,478 pints, which is more than all local residents—Chinese, British and Indians—combined.

American women have contributed too. The American Women's Association raised $9,118.45 in 1961, by selling decorations and charging admissions for teas. Women who have never seen Hong Kong—the Catholic Women's League —formed Operation China Doll in the United States and marketed 25,000 economically priced cloth dolls made by Hong Kong's refugee women.

On the large agency scale, however, the remarkably smooth interplay ironically exists in a colony that was previously involved in constant religious strife instigated by both Catholics *vs.* Protestants and British *vs.* Chinese.

A typical transformation can be found today at the Maryknoll Sisters' Poor School. "These cookies and dried peaches the children are eating," a Sister pointed out, "were donated by the Church World Service. It gave fifty cases of them to every agency. There's just so much to do that there isn't any time for prejudice. It would be an injustice to say that Maryknoll has contributed more than a tiny part."

Church World Service,[2] a prime example of generous American volunteer agencies, is headquartered in one of Kowloon's largest buildings on Prince Edward Road. It is staffed by forty-eight salaried, full-time employees and hundreds of part-time workers.

In 1962, Church World Service was distributing regular relief supplies such as rice, tinned pork and noodles to 128,000 Hong Kong refugees a month; it additionally pro-

[2] A central department of the National Council of Churches of Christ in America, devoted to providing a ministry of relief and rehabilitation to the needy. The Hong Kong branch has representatives from six denominational groups.

vides milk and hot soup to 70,000 children daily at nine stations. The agency operates two tuberculosis clinics, a mobile dental clinic that handles an average of 875 patients a month, a home for orphan girls, the Faith-Hope Nursery School, a blind-teaching project, a student aid project, a foundling home, and of course in Hong Kong a noodle factory that runs two shifts a day.

Church World Service has distributed tons of clothing received through the United States Navy's Operation Hand-clasp, has erected 900 permanent refugee cottages, distributed large quantities of medicines donated by Americans, and in 1962 added a forty-bed male ward to the Haven of Hope Hospital.

It is directed by Reverend Elbert E. Gates, a cheerful, bald-headed Baptist pastor from New Jersey. He and his wife work tirelessly and effectively. Mrs. Gates, who, the American Consulate says, "overflows with goodwill," is closely concerned with handknitting, necktie, smocking and quilting projects, and organized a sweater drive that collected 40,000 sweaters from all over the world.

Doctor Gates started to recall his Hong Kong experiences for an interviewer one day, but the phone rang, and like hundreds of religious workers in the British colony, he had emergency business. The errand was typical of the entries in the diary he keeps:

"*October 26*—After usual office duties and routine, I took the Star ferry to the Hong Kong side of the harbor for two meetings. As I got off the ferry I noticed a large circle

of people. I went over to investigate, and to my utter amaze-
ment found 47 beleaguered people squatting down in Oriental fashion, looking like animals at bay. They were shab-
bily dressed, mostly in rags. None of them wore shoes, and
all of them showed the effects of malnutrition. I asked who
they were, and found they were refugees who had just
arrived from Red China. They had come at night in a junk
from Swatow, 90 miles up the coast.

"It was evident that they were completely bewildered,
and nobody seemed in a position to help them. Although I
couldn't speak their dialect, I broke through the circle of
onlookers, and by means of signs told them I would help
them if they would follow me. After some hesitation, they
decided they could trust me, and so we began the trek
across the harbor to Kowloon, and then the three-mile
journey to the office of Church World Service.

"Almost immediately I could feel the sympathy of the
community as I sought to help these people. When I told
the Star ferry attendants about them, they helped me get
the large group through the turnstiles. Upon arrival in
Kowloon, I had no alternative but to take them on Public
Bus No. 8 for the journey to the office. Two police officers helped me get them aboard. Not having enough money
in my pocket to pay the fares of so many people, I explained
to the conductor, and he smilingly waived collection of the
fares which were beyond my resources. Two passengers,
seeing my predicament, helped me get the refugees off the
bus and up to the office.

"Fortunately one of our staff members could speak their dialect, and so we were able to establish communications. They told of a terrible hunger, and pitifully asked for food. I immediately took them to a nearby Chinese restaurant, and allowed them to eat as much as they wanted. Seldom have I seen people eat so avidly. They had second and third helpings. In fact, they cleaned out the restaurant. They said they hadn't seen food like that in years.

"In the meantime, I called Rev. Hugh Smith, an American Baptist missionary who also speaks the Swatow dialect. With Mr. Smith acting as the interpreter, we began to learn their story.

"They were seven families, including several young people and children. They had been living in a commune outside the city of Swatow. Although they were not farming people, they had been forced to work on farms. They started early in the morning before breakfast and worked until dark. In the evening, they were compelled to go to meetings for indoctrination by the Communist authorities. They were not paid for their work, but received food through the communes consisting of four taels of rice a day for the adults, and as little as one tael per day for small children. They were granted sixteen feet of cloth a year for clothing.

"With life so harsh, they decided to try to make an escape. First, plans were made as far back as June. One of their number got hold of a junk—a Chinese fishing vessel commonly used along the China coast—and although it was difficult to make plans because of close police surveillance, they managed to arrange a rendezvous at midnight on October 24, on the edge of Swatow Harbor. Fortunately their plans worked, and they made their escape, even taking along two teenage girls who saw them in flight and begged to be taken. They had no opportunity to bid farewell to their families.

"After the meal at the restaurant, I took them back to the office, where we made plans for the night. Several had ugly-looking sores, and so we called upon Dr. Kenneth Tsang, a local physician, to treat them. We then headed for our Chuk Yuen Community Center, where temporary living quarters could be provided.

"It was a revealing experience to note their reactions during the journey to Chuk Yuen. By then it was dark. They had never seen such bright lights, nor had they seen so many shops. When we reached the Community Center high on the hillside above the city, they fairly cried with joy at the beauty of the lights stretched out before them.

"It was also heart-warming to see how they were welcomed by the Chinese staff at the center. The caretaker Abiyah had made his escape only a year previously, and he was so overjoyed at their miraculous deliverance he said he would cook for them as long as was necessary. Other staff members joyfully welcomed them and began to help them find locations on floors in the classrooms where they could bed down for the night. We were able to give each person a blanket from our stores in the Church World Service warehouse. Also toilet articles.

"By this time, word had spread among the refugees living in the shacks on the hillside that new refugees had arrived. Within minutes, clothing was arriving which the residents had collected and could ill afford to share, but eloquent testimony to the fundamental goodness of human nature.

"It was now 10 o'clock in the evening, and they began to think of sleep. We assured them we would do all within our power to help them get started in their new life. Before leaving, we had a brief time of prayer together when we asked God to bless these homeless people, to give them the physical and spiritual strength needed for their ordeal, and to help us to be able to reveal God's love to them through our own loving hands and hearts. Tears streamed down their faces for the first time, and one of the men said, 'We have never known such love from strangers.'

"When I drove home with my wife and daughter, it was nearly 11 o'clock. None of us had had dinner, and we were dead tired, but we knew we had lived through a day which will seldom be equalled in our lives, a day when we had been able to express love and compassion and friendliness to a group of desperate people in the very midst of their ordeal."

"*November 3*—Fifty-four refugees arrived this morning from China. They are still on the junk and four sampans in which they came. Their physical condition is poor and . . ."

Church World Service, like Maryknoll or Catholic Relief Services, could fill a volume. And it might take an equal volume for the Lutheran World Service. The Lutherans are engaged in the same refugee projects—noodles and all—plus courses in tailoring and porcelain painting. They also operate one of the only two general hospitals in the New Territories, have rehabilitation programs, and combat drug addiction—no incidental problem in Hong Kong. The Lutherans' drug drive has been augmented by the Christian Welfare and Relief Council, which totals a membership of twenty-four leading churches and Christian agencies in Hong Kong. It disbursed about $2,760,000 during 1961. The donations came from everywhere—from Malaya to Germany, from Holland to New Zealand.

Although Hong Kong's charity contribution goes in cycles, the immensity of the problem usually prevents duplication. Much of this unity has developed from the Hong Kong Council of Social Services, which is administered from David House by Executive Secretary Madge Newcombe. This farsighted group, founded in 1936, was necessitated by refugees escaping Japanese armies in South China, then reorganized and enlarged in 1950, when the Chinese ran from the Communists. It not only coordinates smaller agencies, but utilizes the tourist trade. When a newcomer leaves the Star ferry on the Kowloon side for a cab or rickshaw—or walks up Salisbury Road to the Peninsula or Ambassador hotels—it is impossible to miss the Refugee Welfare Handicraft Shop. It offers everything from hand-painted Chinese scrolls to men's pajamas.

And the visitor will probably be handed a three-page pamphlet with this type of question:

*Are you interested in what is being done for children?* Get in touch with the Maryknoll Sisters, Shatin Babies' Home, or Christian Children's Fund, Inc.

*Hospitals?* Try American Presbyterian Mission Casework Center [and a page of others].

*Old People?* Cannossian Mission Delegation or West China Evangelistic Band [and the list goes on, down to such familiar names as CARE and the Salvation Army].

Miss Newcombe distributed a set of cards that are designed to help needy beggars and thwart professionals. If a beggar approaches one of her workers, he is handed a card stating: IF YOU GO TO ONE OF THE WELFARE ORGANIZATIONS LISTED ON THE BACK OF THIS CARD, THEY WILL DO THEIR BEST TO INVESTIGATE YOUR NEEDS AND HELP YOU.

Professional beggars, conservatively estimated at 10,000 in Hong Kong, stand in alleys and shove out seven- and eight-year-old children carrying babies to stimulate pity. Beggars follow tourists and tug at their clothing for blocks. They back off when they get a card.

While children do roam the streets, they certainly are not neglected. Even if the following newspaper item (in complete text) is routine:

> Two baby girls, one about a month old and the other about three months, have been found. The one-month-old girl was found abandoned on Kwong Fuk Road, and the other infant was found in a public lavatory.

Babies are abandoned daily and orphanages are clogged. A nursery orphanage a few yards from Father Edmonds' Chai Wan parish is operated by the British Commonwealth Save the Children Fund from money raised by the Hong

Kong Junior Chamber of Commerce's "Miss International Beauty Contest of 1961."

The Christian Children's Fund operates homes accommodating 1,236 children and assists in projects caring for an additional 3,923. And the Jesuits help many more orphan boys by providing them with a credit union, quarters, meals and the rudiments of education at their Wah Yan College.

There are schools to fit the needs. Across from some chicken crates refugees call "home" in a smelly area of Aberdeen Bay is the Aberdeen Trade School. Built by a Chinese committee and entrusted to the Salesian Fathers, this school boards and instructs 383 boys in becoming electricians, mechanics, draftsmen and instructors. And there's a waiting list at the Hong Kong Sea School, which trains and disciplines around 175 boys annually to work on ships as seamen, stewards or firemen.

Helping hands were needed in unexpected fields—even fishing, which not only is Hong Kong's but also mankind's oldest industry. The easiest way to escape from Communist China is by boat, and the fishing population around Aberdeen's "Junk City," Shau Ki and the outlying island of Cheung Chau, swelled to 150,000. The *tonga* (water people), who are born and raised on their little wooden junks and have a 99 percent illiteracy, could not meet the fishing competition; there were just too many people fishing and selling at cheaper prices.

There were naturally fewer fish to catch as schools of them moved farther out to sea. The fishermen could not sail far enough in a day to catch them. Since there was not

164

a single mechanized junk in Aberdeen Bay when the refugee tide began, that put them at the mercy of another vice. Fishermen who did venture farther out did not have facilities for preserving their catches and were compelled to sell the same day or throw the fish overboard the next day. So the *laans* (wholesalers) paid the fishermen just what they wanted to pay them. Then, during typhoons and off seasons they would advance the fishermen small sums of money at such exorbitant rates of interest that the people were hopelessly in debt and some even lost their floating huts. It resembled a Prohibition era "juice racket" of moneylending.

The situation was improved considerably by an innovation of Father J. P. McCarthy's, an Irish Jesuit teacher, and cooperation with the Hong Kong government. Father McCarthy pioneered the Fishing Marketing Organization, a purchasing cooperative. Refugees who were unable to sell directly to legitimate markets organized five wholesale markets where fish were sorted to size and type, weighed and sold at daily auctions.

Working with government funds, Father McCarthy launched a credit-union procedure to purchase boating equipment, nets or repairs. As the project materialized he tried another "experiment" on a volunteer named Lai Kwong Chau. A motor was installed on his junk, allowing him to fish several miles from shore. It drew crowds comparable to those of the first horseless carriage. By 1962 there were 3,500 mechanized vessels off Hong Kong.

Temporary schooling was introduced to fishing families in 1951, and one of the first graduates was Lai Kwok Kui, son of a Cheung Chau fisherman, who graduated from the University of Tokyo Fisheries School in 1962. He then returned, to work with Hong Kong's research division ship *Cape Queen Mary*, which is extending into marine biology and oceanography to introduce information on better fishing.

Farmland also became a problem. Even "the good earth," as Chinese land became known through Pearl Buck's novel about a Chinese farmer, is not very good in the part of China called Hong Kong. That's why Hong Kong was sold originally. Much of its 398½ acres is mountainous or rocky. When a Chinese in Kowloon brags that he owns "a farm," a close inspection sometimes reveals that he has only what an American farmer would call a few yards of arable land.

Land was indeed badly needed in Hong Kong, which depends largely on Red China for water, meat and vegetables. While land was too precious for another Maryknoll cottage in Kowloon, it was also too scarce for antiquated farming thirty-five miles farther back in the New Territories. The Agriculture and Forestry Department encouraged anything improving crop and animal quality so strongly that it virtually gave away fertilizer. And, as many expelled missionaries wanted to help, it sponsored a project headed by a well-known Irish Jesuit, Father Thomas Ryan, who was assisted by Robert Hart, a British businessman from North China. They not only organized vegetable and marketing cooperatives—which swelled to over 70 cooperatives and 5,000 members by 1961—but introduced new plowing and harrowing methods. The good land which was capable of irrigation could provide two rice crops a year, and lower portions of mountains and hillsides could be terraced for such fringe benefits as sweet potatoes and sugar cane.

There were many individual contributors too. Among them were two brothers, Lawrence and Horace Kadoorie, who gave $43,750—equaled by the government—to purchase 10,000 acres of marginal land that became a model refugee farming cooperative. Competition became so keen in animal husbandry that the 1961 animal show pulled 5,500 entries—everything from water buffalo (the Chinese tractor) to hogs.

A man named Gus Borgheest, another British layman, took $2,000 and twelve refugee families to one of the virtually uncultivable islands, and the 180-acre tract became known as Sunshine Island. His ingenious trick—a simple poultry cooperative. It is such a fine example of man's desire to live without Communism that Borgheest received the Philippine Government's Magsaysay Award—Asia's equivalent to the Nobel Peace Prize.

# 14.

## UNINVITED PARTNER

**H**ONG KONG has a "partner." When the colony's borders tighten, refugees slip in at night from the "depot" in nearby Macao,[1] the stolid Portuguese enclave three and a half hours away by boat on the Pearl River's south bank.

Nothing seems to disturb Macao's tranquil existence. Nothing seems to change. It can't expand; it can never become a major port. The harbor is too shallow. Macao is unaltered by war and politics. Even Japanese soldiers didn't bother to occupy it completely during World War II.

Today it has few automobiles or industries. There is little work for the 400,000 population—many of whom are temporary refugees—except making firecrackers. But its

---

[1] The minimum fee is $9 per refugee.

centuries-old *status quo*, unsophistication, and banyan-lined streets preserve its Mediterranean charm. A common sight is a water buffalo in one lane and a man driving a cart pulled by his wife in the other; or a man shadowboxing in the street.

In Macao, everything can happen and does. Its international notoriety stems from pulp-magazine publicity about the girls on the Rúa da Felicidade (Happiness Alley), roulette, opium, smuggling and illegal gold traffic. While some cases may have been exaggerated, they remain relatively true.

Macao's purpose is unchanging. China ceded it to Portugal about 1557, as reimbursement for eliminating pirates in the area. The Communists could seize it any time—as India took the Portuguese enclave of Goa. But China still uses Macao for exporting undesirables. As Harry Anslinger, recently retired United States Commissioner of Narcotics, says, Communist China ships most of its opium through Macao. And while Macao remains a proud sanctuary for refugees, the Communists issue exit permits to the aged and mentally sick, allowing them to stroll through the arched gate of Portas do Cerco and into Macao. Simultaneously a daily occurrence is Chinese sampans trying to outrace Communist gunboats to Macao.

These refugees need help, and the tapestry of the past continues to be woven in Macao. For centuries its biggest hero was the Jesuit Father who fired the cannon from Fort do Monte at an invading Dutch fleet. Today two of its heroes are Jesuit priests: Father Luis Ruiz, a good-natured Spaniard who operates a Catholic Relief Services outlet and refugee center in a rundown villa named Casa Ricci; and Father Launcelot Rodriguez—a lively priest who carries a guitar on his motor scooter and enjoys pepping up crowds with sidewalk serenades.

Macao too benefits from Monsignor Romaniello's popular noodle experiments. "There are plenty of places in the world," the monsignor said in Macao, "that don't have electricity to run noodle machines. Like Tibet, India, Vietnam and these little islands around Macao. But you've still got to feed people."

Macao has electricity, but Taipa, one of its two islands (1.3 square miles and 6,000 people) does not. Monsignor Romaniello wanted to inspect his Taipa noodle project, so he, Major Sigismundo Reves, Police Commissioner of Macao, Father Rodriguez and others climbed into a chipped Portuguese marine boat for the twenty-minute ride, passing the dingy blue Communist gunboat No. 4036 that later the same night shot three young boys trying to escape. The group was greeted by Pinto Cardso, a police inspector, near a century-old cannon. The impish monsignor manned the cannon and quipped, "Hey, Mr. Mao, look here! *Boom!*"

They all climbed into a jeep and traveled through swampy land past grass-thatched huts, finally stopping at a contrasting three acres that had been filled in, complete with a concrete archway and a four-foot rock fence. It is what Communists publicize as a prison. But if it weren't for Red China, there'd be no need for it. It is a rehabilitation center that was originated by Major Reves, a husky, thirty-nine-year-old ex-soccer player from Lisbon who came to Macao as commissioner in 1961. His explanation: "Here and at our other places we have—today's count—four hundred and fifty men and twenty-seven women who have come out of Communist China. They're not bad, but they're not good either. They aren't going to improve by begging, smoking opium and petty stealing. They haven't any chance for jobs, and here they can spend six months learning trades like bricklaying or sewing. Moreover, they not only feed themselves but other refugees."

In the first building housing Monsignor Romaniello's experiment a man made dough in a shiny washtub, then carried it to twelve men operating hand-cranked noodle machines. They each produced 150 pounds of noodles daily, which fed 900 people.

"We gave Major Reves twelve machines just three months ago," said the monsignor, with his infectious broad smile, "and the results are self-evident. This is what can be done for the rest of Asia, Africa, South America and all backward places."

In the beginning Major Reves had received more criticism than praise, since local opinion held that there was no need for anything new. But when Reves realized the kind of people the Communists were shoving over the border, he launched his plans. Even the police ignored orders to round up criminals, only occasionally arresting one or two. Reves issued a firm order, and the police brought in 400 at one time. Insiders claimed it to be a scheme to overload the major with prisoners so he would drop the plan. But he didn't, and it has proven highly practical.

When the group stopped to visit a work supervisor, Father Rodriguez volunteered an example of its success. "Major Reves won't brag on his own project," he said, "but one man he brought here to learn bricklaying got a job in Hong Kong recently and mailed back five dollars as a donation to 'help someone else get arrested like him.'"

Then the jeep weaved in and out and cut around sharp corners and narrow European-type streets en route to other rehabilitation areas. Monsignor Romaniello, sitting in the front seat, said, "Major Reves certainly has done a lot to help these people. Holds charity football games and even plays himself."

They pulled to a stop and faced a growling dog which appeared confident enough to eat jeep and passengers too.

"Huh," snapped Cardso, a mustached, blue-uniformed Portuguese who normally doesn't speak English. "That dog is a Communist. No mistake about that."

But the dog was bluffing, and they climbed out safely and puffed up a steep incline to a once-deserted, yellow seafront building that had been painted trimly and converted. Men pedaling sewing machines and making uniforms were listening to music from a transistor radio; others were pounding coconut shells into broom fibers, and becoming skillful in things they could apply later on when they escaped to Hong Kong.

The jeep pulled to the top of another hill and an abandoned army barracks. Two hundred men were moving a mountain—digging and chiseling away at a hillside—to make room for a new building. They used the dirt to fill in the ocean, while the rocks were hammered into gravel.

Mental institutions had refused many of these men because they were hopeless cases and because there is no room, since Communist China is flooding tiny Macao with the sick. And the number of mentally broken is rising as Communist harshness increases.

One man stopped to say, "I used to be the Number One Pirate in all China. Number One, I tell you."

"That's wonderful," Monsignor Romaniello said softly. "If you're going to be anything, you might as well be something big—Number One in your field."

A ninety-two-year-old woman stood idle. But it was better than sleeping in the streets and begging; the only food she got in China was what she stole.

"I used to be bad," she explained excitedly, "but I wanted to be good. I have to steal in China. But God has helped. Even if I stay in China I be bad, because all Communism is bad."

Down the hill the others were just as industrious in turning the little island into a showplace. "Out there"—Monsignor Romaniello pointed—"is the same water that laps Mao Tsetung's place. But here is progress. These are people who were picked up for dead."

# 15.

## THE SHIFTY SET

SINCE the public exposure of Communist China's crimes basically originates in Hong Kong, why do the Communists permit the worldwide embarrassment of Hong Kong to continue? This is the same Red regime that has openly declared World War III. Every move, regardless of its size, is calculated as another step toward conquering the world. If they cannot seize half or all of a country—such as Tibet, Korea, Laos, or Vietnam—they peck away at yardage; every day they creep farther on the China-India border. And Hong Kong is a colony and they could "liberate the Chinese people from the imperialist West" with a phone call.

According to intelligence reports, the Communists have never seriously considered a move against Hong Kong.

What convinced them was the transformation of Shanghai, once the "Hong Kong of the Orient," into a ghost port under their regime. A cliché fits—taking Hong Kong would be like locking themselves in and throwing away the key.

Each year Communist China receives between $85 and $90 million from sales, mostly food, in Hong Kong. Its annual international payments, or entire foreign exchange, also is between $85 and $90 million. The tragedy is that many starving people in China raise food they are not allowed to eat. Two-thirds of every crop is collected by the government, and when a drought comes, as it has frequently during the past few years, people must go hungry. The thousands who evacuated Kwangtung province for Hong Kong in May of 1962 were fed with rice they had raised but which had been sold to that colony.

The post office can give statistical verification of the growing famine in China. In 1959, Hong Kong residents mailed 870,000 two-pound food packages to Communist China; in 1960, they mailed 3,700,000. In 1961, they sent 13,302,500. Half the postage collected in Hong Kong is for packages to China. During the first three months of 1962, Hong Kong's postage revenue was $3,109,438.50; foodstuffs to China amounted to $1,629,867. Every post-office branch has special signs, PACKETS TO CHINA, and lines extend into the streets. Many Hong Kong donors must lighten their packages, since there is a two-pound limit. A well-circulated joke is, "Well, the Red postal workers must be too weak from starvation to lift any more."

Occasionally some of this food is American surplus distributed by Maryknoll and Americans. However, the tax is so exorbitant that many people never receive it. In fact, the Communists confiscated so much food from persons unable to pay the duty—usually 200 to 300 percent of the value— that they constructed a huge warehouse on their side of the Lowu border in which to store it.

Therefore most food donors are forced to use the Communist gimmick. In Hong Kong there are about 3,000 shops which are known to be dealing with Communist China, but only about 50 stores—headed by the China Products Company—offer the "special." Instead of buying food, paying postage and taxes, the donor simply buys a ticket in Hong Kong, and the China recipient exchanges it for food at a slightly larger value than if the food had been purchased outside. This means that the Communists won't allow people to eat their own food unless an outsider pays for it.

Periodically, Communist-sponsored advertisements soliciting such methods of sending food to China appear in Hong Kong's Chinese-language newspapers. One newspaper, the English-language Hong Kong *Tiger Standard*, ran this article in its September 26, 1961, edition:

> The Chinese Communists have come out with a new gimmick to encourage local residents to remit more money to the mainland.
>
> The bait is the hope of providing a little more food for starving relatives on the China mainland.
>
> The new Chinese Communist call is for local residents to treat their relatives on the mainland to a "banquet," but while the food is to be served on the mainland, payment is to be made here and in advance.

Coupons of $20 [$3.50] are on sale at Chinese Communist banks in Hong Kong. These coupons are to be mailed to relatives on the mainland.

Any family on the mainland who accumulates 10 coupons worth a total of $200HK [$35] will be entitled to a banquet in a public dining hall.

Those who do not have as many as 10 may, however, register with a public dining hall and then wait for other recipients to register their coupons to make up the requisite number and share the banquet with them.

As to the quality of the feast in store for $200HK, the Chinese Communists have discreetly kept the menu a top secret.

Most people are at the mercy of the Communist ruse of purchasing food inside China. Witnesses regularly testify that the Communists allow food parcels to rot on railway sidings. Several men and women returning from Canton described this situation as "terrible." The campaign is reinforced by harassing searches and special additional taxes at the Lowu border.

One particular case familiar to Monsignor Romaniello had a somewhat humorous aspect. An English-speaking Communist guard discovered an illiterate refugee carrying a yellow noodle bag with the inscription, A GIFT FROM THE PEOPLE OF THE UNITED STATES. And the food was wrapped in a Sunday issue of *Stars and Stripes,* the overseas American Army daily. The man was arrested for "trying to overthrow the country," but finally was released when it was established that he couldn't even read his own name.

Chinese Communist strategy in Hong Kong has been overhauled since 1952, and it contrasts with their previous operations there and elsewhere. It first followed the working manuals with plots like: "How To Storm the U. S. Embassy in Tokyo," or "How To Burn the American Flag in Caracas," or incite "A Riot that Suggests Anti-West Sentiment." It followed that line in Hong Kong, as Father Trube learned soon after he moved into the Tung Tau Tsuen squatter camp damaged by fire.

On May Day, 1952, the Communists sent a "comfort mission" from Canton, ostensibly to distribute a few gifts and propaganda, although they were aware that Hong Kong authorities would not approve entrance visas of known agitators and that they would be stranded at the Lowu border. So the Communists staged a union demonstration at the Kowloon railroad station. It festered into a screaming mob which stormed past the Peninsula Hotel, mauling foreigners and burning cars on its march up Nathan Road. The objects of their "affection," the fire victims of Tung Tau Tsuen, were studiously avoided.

In the beginning, the Communists' biggest demonstration was scheduled every October 1, the anniversary of the founding of the Party. Members were compelled to show Party love by flying flags or decorating buildings. By 1962, the demonstration had dwindled to a virtually insignificant event. "Around my area," Father Rielly pointed out, "there were flags on a Commie school, of course, and maybe a couple more on some little shops. But that's all."

Only 731 Communist flags and 64 decorated façades appeared on all of Hong Kong's islands and boats during the 1961 anniversary; it was celebrated quietly, by reporting the "great advances in China" to a crowd and press party announced as 1,700. The story was carried under a one-column headline on the back page. A well-timed article in the October 1 issue of the *Tiger Standard*, under a two-column headline on Page 1, read: STARVATION PREVAILS IN CHINA MAINLAND, DEFECTOR TELLS PRESS. A short follow-up reported that "the Soviet Union had dispatched a low-level delegation to Communist China."

It was an about-face on October 10, which is called "Double Tenth," meaning the 10th day of the 10th month marking the founding of Nationalist China. "This same area that had maybe two or three Communist flags the week before," Father Trube said, "had six to seven thousand Nationalist flags that day."

The Nationalists' popularity was overwhelming. The colony resembled a Christmas scene, and the October 11 issue of the *Tiger Standard* reported it on Page 1 with this three-column headline and a four-column picture: MILLION FLAGS MARK N'LIST DAY HERE. No one doubted that there were at least a million flags, but the informed found amusement in the *Tiger Standard*, with its 8,200 daily circulation, claiming it had counted every flag.[1]

Openly, Communism has no appreciable standing in Hong Kong. All relief and church groups—not only Maryknoll—

---

[1] The paper gave this tabulation: On Hong Kong Island, it reported 624 decorative façades, 8,089 cloth flags and 285,029 paper flags; in the suburbs, it counted 53 decorative façades, 354 cloth and 27,121 paper flags; in the urban area of Kowloon, it recorded 623 decorative façades, 495,684 paper and 14,149 cloth flags. On the New Territories and Islands it found 259 decorative façades, 3,821 cloth flags and 108,238 paper flags. There were 30 flower plaques, 731 cloth and 63,002 paper flags for a total of 1,006,228.

strongly maintain: "The Communists have very little toe hold in our area." And it's evident. But these groups are working with the poor refugee who has been burned by Communism, and his sentiment is so strong that he wants to go back with a Nationalist landing party. It supports a theory that anyone who has tasted Communism's interworkings would never choose it again.

Not everyone, however, has experienced it, and Communism seems to be firmly established in Hong Kong. But not everyone believes this. Communist support may be listed in this manner:

1. *The British,* who recognize Communist China and walk a tightrope, not openly offending the Communists, but quietly trying to suppress any growth that endangers the colony.

2. *Traders and exporters* who insist: "I'm not here to talk politics. I'm here to do business and make money." Consequently many, including Americans, have risen from nothing to millionaire status. Many of them own the boats that load only at night, or transfer to a middleman who then wheels and deals for the Communists. One intelligence report states that a scrapped American warship went directly into China.

3. *The middle class,* which inwardly hates Communists, but is blackmailed into silence for fear of retaliation against relatives in China.

4. *Children* ignorant of Communism's real intent—the prime target of such propaganda.

5. *Genuine Communists and Communist supporters,* who mingle and, if necessary, say, "I'm anti-Communist," to make inroads.

6. *Communist agents.*

Instead of getting on the platform and screaming, as before, the Communists now grow by minimizing attention. They are no doubt firmly intrenched. Until the new city hall was completed in 1961, Hong Kong Island's tallest building was the Communist-owned Bank of China, one of five which the Reds own. They indirectly control four smaller banks.

The Hong Kong Communist system is highly organized and begins with the local central committee, which is responsible for training, in strikes, riots, etc. The agency is compartmentalized into:

1. The seamen and ferry workers
2. Commerce
3. Agriculture
4. The fishermen
5. Labor Unions
6. Education
7. Colleges
8. Clubs
9. Cultural events
10. Financial
11. Transportation
12. Political affairs

The Hong Kong Federal Trade Union, which backs Communism, has 63 affiliated unions, mostly in textile mills, shipping or ships, and public utilities, plus 28 other independent unions considered left-wing. The rival Hong Kong and Kowloon Trade Council, with 66 affiliates and 55 independent unions, leans toward the Nationalists. It consists mainly of construction and catering personnel and has a large membership, but the paid-up and active list is lower.

Communist intelligence embraces American tourists, local residents, diplomats, military personnel; and has departments for the local Chinese, overseas Chinese, Taiwan Chinese, British, etc. Charming hostesses are brazen about seeking information. Some have reported being forced to work as agents or lose their parents in China. In October 1961, there were reports that the Hong Kong government had pierced a major Communist spy ring. A few days later the government deported John Tsang, Hong Kong Assistant Police Superintendent, for spying. One of his responsibilities had been to apprehend refugee smugglers from Macao. Another officer caught him receiving, from a refugee, an envelope which initially was thought to be a bribe, but turned out to be a Communist spy message. Today John Tsang is employed in Canton as an official of the Chinese Public Security Force and as *special advisor on Hong Kong and Macao operations.*

The Red propaganda department has alarming newspaper strength. There are 4 English- and 39 Chinese-language papers in Hong Kong with a total circulation of 768,000. The Communists have 10 Chinese-language papers, led by the *Shang Pao* (Hong Kong *Commercial Daily*), and a combined 1962 circulation of 189,000—an increase of 24,300 over 1961. While scoring circulation gains, the papers suffered a different loss when Eric Chou, an editor and secretary to the publisher of the pro-Red *Ta Kung Pao* newspaper defected.

Only three newspapers—*Shang Pao, Ching Po Daily* and *Ming Po*—made a profit, and the remainder required Communist subsidy. Most papers avoid circulation gimmicks such as crossword puzzles and quiz contests, but *Ming Po's* substantial circulation gain was credited to the addition of horse-racing tips and "love" series.

Typical features in the political papers are, THE EVIL DEEDS OF THE AMERICAN CONSULATE IN HONG KONG DURING THE PAST 10 YEARS. "Many ugly plots," it reported, "including those of subversive nature were discovered. The USIS in Hong Kong was among the lucky ones, but it made a fool of itself just the same."

There are 27 pro-Communist magazines, with a total monthly circulation of 332,500,[2] although many are not stable. One of those that folded in 1961 was the *Hsiang Tu* (*Native Land*), a news magazine reporting on nearby Kwangtung province. When it failed to mention that virtually the entire province was rioting for food, even Hong Kong Communists quit buying it. But it was replaced by the *Little Children's Playground*, which quickly reached a circulation of 22,000. Most of the publications are primed for a particular audience, such as the *Teacher's Monthly*, which has 3,500 subscribers, and the student-aimed *Youth's Garden*, which distributes 13,000 weekly.

The Communist's top publishing strength is in books. They have revised their thinking here too. Previously they flooded the market with low-priced books that nobody read. Now they are concentrating on quality, aiming for the ten-to-fifteen-year-old audience. They published 300 so-called major books in 1961. There were only 80 non-Communist

---

[2] As a comparison, there is a total of 47 non-Communist publications with a circulation of 673,900.

books printed during the same year, and 11 of these came from the United States' World Press Today, Hong Kong's largest non-Communist publisher.

Pro-Communist publishers and distributors outnumber non-Communist so heavily—107 to 35—that they don't have enough books to go around. Oddly enough, four Communist shops resorted to selling books published in Taiwan in 1961, to keep operating. Most publishers and distributors are united with front organizations, subsidiaries and affiliates. While the largest are the Commercial Press, World Publishing Company, and Shanghai Book Company, leftists use such names as "Peace Book Store," "Chinese Emigrants' Book Company," "Full Wind," "Happiness," "Knowledge," and "New Learning."

The morale of the Communist movie crowd, however, is obviously low. This is largely because of the defection of two top actors and the decline of the Grandview Studio, where the pro-Communist Great Wall Company filmed most of its pictures.

There had been prior failures. Miss Chung Sui-Ming, who supervised Communist films in Hong Kong, was pulled back late in 1961 for her lack of success. There was so much rewriting on the Communist approach that top pictures were rejected by the Red Chinese. They didn't contain enough propaganda. Later the Communists realized that they would capture larger audiences by improving the pictures' artistic value and softening their violent propaganda approach. Consequently they carefully blended indoctrination into a color epic called *Women Generals in the Yang Family*, which was based on an old Peiping opera. It set a record (65,565) for a Mandarin film. They have little difficulty showing Communist films; of 16 Communist Chinese 35-mm pictures screened by censors during one period, 13 were approved, 2 passed with cuts, and only one was banned.

The five pro-Communist theatres [3] have been losing money since the United States blacklisted them. The Astor, for example, is limited to showing Chinese, Russian, Czech and Italian pictures. And since Hong Kong is a British colony, all first- and second-run houses are compelled to show 10 percent British films.

All in all, Communist China uses Hong Kong for its department store and sounding board; and it goes on down to smaller needs. There is such a shortage of gasoline that none is wasted in training bus drivers; forty were recruited from Hong Kong. Another time, it pulled out 300 mechanics. One of the mechanics wrote a friend: "My biggest mistake was not bringing a hammer with me to beat myself."

Anyone living in Hong Kong long enough cannot escape the fear that he is at Communist China's mercy. Some permanent American residents claim they have been told that ships and planes are always available to evacuate them. You hear, too, that British intelligence can detect any Communist movement. While this undoubtedly is true, it doesn't do much good. The British not only pulled out their navy and closed the dockyards, but also suggested the withdrawal of the token garrison force.

This created a controversy among British politicians. On

[3] The Cathay, the largest, the Liberty, Kuo Shing, Astor and Star.

March 9, 1962, George Wigg, a prominent Labor back-bencher, stood up in England's House of Commons and criticized statements that Britain could not defend Hong Kong, and suggested that all forces be withdrawn. A name-calling argument resulted. "I have tried to be rude," Wigg said, "and shall continue to be rude when people play politics with soldiers' lives."

It probably doesn't make much difference whether England withdraws the garrison or not. Some British soldiers apparently are as demoralized as the bushy-headed kid who dropped 6 cents into a juke box, punched THE TWIST, U.S.A., and sat back down with his draft beer.

"We're sent to Hong Kong for three years, and the only way you can go home," he began, "is marry a rich girl. Here we're supposed to be protecting the British, but they look down their noses and regard us as scum. Of course, there's probably a little of that in every country, but you can say, 'We're soldiers and the hell with it.' But the hell of it is we'd all get wiped out if the Communists did come over the hill. We only get thirty practice rounds of ammo a year. If the Commies started a fight, we have seven thousand tons of ammo, and that's enough to hold out maybe forty-eight hours. And it's a five-day ship ride from Singapore to bring in any extras."

The kid worked in the ammo dump.

But perhaps the British High Command figured the Chinese Communists would never attack that way. Why would they start a fight, when—after all—they could simply poison the water they pipe into Hong Kong?

# 16.

## MISSION IN HELL

THE fortunes of Maryknoll and Chinese Communism have been intertwined since the beginning of both organizations. In 1920, two years after Maryknoll had begun its first China mission in the walled town of Yeungkong, another group was laying a foundation to bring Communism to the world's largest nation.

Two Russian agents and seven Chinese grouped around Professor Ch'en Tu Hsiu in a small printshop and persuaded Ch'en to slant his *New Youth* magazine toward Soviet ideas. The following year twelve Communists met in an unused American school in Shanghai for their first congress.

Maryknoll and the Communists were soon rivals. Maryknoll urged religious colleagues to consider the need for a new thinking toward the Chinese, while the Communists called for a different attitude toward foreigners in China. Neither was initially successful.

Subsequently, Communist agents made copious notes, compiling a complete dossier on Maryknoll's work in China. In the twisted logic of Marxist-Leninism, the Communists later began publicizing the Maryknoll personnel. They claimed that the twelve Maryknoll missionaries who had died in China were there only for evil deeds and to exploit the people. The Communist word had gained authority by late 1949, when the tough Red troops were also utilizing the "Human-sea suicide assaults," were taking town after town from the Nationalists, and were soon in Maryknoll's mission territory.

Many of the priests who manned the missions—usually older than the Fathers who were to pioneer the Hong Kong work—suffered heavily.

There was usually a ten-day lull, following Communist victories, before their police, Party workers and new government arrived.

From Shanghai, where he was under house arrest as director of the nation's Catholic Central Bureau, Bishop James Edward Walsh wrote:

> It is the plain duty of all Catholic missionaries, priests, Brothers and Sisters, regardless of age, occupation or condition, to remain where they are until prevented from doing so by physical force.... Persecution is the normal risk of missionaries, much as in the case of firemen or policemen who are sometimes required to give their lives in fire or robberies.

The Communists agreed and canceled missioners' travel permits.

Bishop Adolph Paschang, prelate of the Kongmoon diocese, ordered all Maryknollers in his area to Kongmoon, so they would be closer to top Communist authorities and beyond reach of uncontrollable young cadres. But Kongmoon, which was Maryknoll's first diocese, was the Communists' opening target.

Phase One involved "cleaning up the town." The Communists executed the landlords, indoctrinated Communism at gunpoint, opened a "Hate America" campaign and adopted a new "religion." The Peking regime announced the formation of a church independent of foreigners, and all Chinese Christians were ordered to join as their "patriotic duty."

Phase Two involved torturing or liquidating Chinese priests and nuns. On July 21, 1951, Fathers Lei, Hong and Hoh—Maryknoll Chinese priests—were tortured severely and publicly exhibited in stocks. Signs around their necks called them "running dogs" of the Americans. All three were sentenced to years of hard labor. One by one all Kongmoon lay teachers and catechists received similar treatment.

Phase Three called for psychological warfare on members of the Maryknoll personnel. They were interrogated daily for a minimum of five hours. Often they were awakened in the middle of the night to endure screaming questioning. In each case, however, the Communists stopped short of murder. They had learned that there was no profit in making foreign martyrs.

The final objective, after all Kongmoon missions were

closed, was to disgrace Bishop Paschang publicly. The Communist Farmers' Union—a political-front organization—held a rally to incite the crowd as it condemned the bishop "for forcing tenant farmers to pay grain taxes for fields adjacent to the mission buildings" and "murdering babies in his orphanage and using their eyes to make medicine." The fields were mission property and no rent had been asked. The bishop was fined for a rebate dating back to 1944, plus 10,000 pounds of unhusked rice.

Afterward Bishop Paschang, his hands tied behind him, was paraded through the streets for two successive days. When he was unable to walk any longer, he was dragged. But Kongmoon residents did not cheer. They knew that his farming techniques and knitting mills had raised the local standard of living; he had helped the poor with rice kitchens and dispensaries. So he was taken to towns where he was not known and where the local militia followed the Communist Farmers' Union's orders by applying an ancient Chinese torture.

A rope was thrown over the bishop's head, the loop knot falling to the back, with two long ends hanging to the ground. The ends were wound around each of his arms above the elbows and jerked tight, pinning his elbows together behind his back. The guard twisted the rope around the bishop's neck until his lips became discolored and his face bloated. When he gasped for breath, the guard released the rope momentarily. But before the bishop could regain complete circulation, the rope was jerked back again. Bishop Paschang would be knocked down and the rope slackened;

then he would be pulled up by the neck. His wrists and knees were rubbed raw, and blood seeped into his shoes.

The Communists offered to release him for $40,000 ransom, but Maryknoll rejected the demand, since it would mean putting every mission in China under similar extortion. The demand was lowered to $22,000. Maryknoll still refused. Finally, exhausted by their own efforts to break the bishop's will and obtain a confession which would discredit Maryknoll, the Communists asked him to apply for an exit permit.

The stubborn little bishop not only refused but registered at Toishan Hospital as an orderly so that there would be no legal excuse to deport him. On June 1, 1952, however, security police informed Bishop Paschang that he had disobeyed the law and was no longer wanted in China. A Communist soldier took him into Macao.[1]

The Communists followed the same technique in Maryknoll's Wuchow diocese. After terrorizing the people, they worked on native priests, nuns and catechists and planted "evidence" for predetermined public trials.

"In Bishop Donaghy's case these Communists ran a well-organized show," said Father Rielly, who was stationed in Wuchow. "The cadres sent in a boy with a gun—unbeknown to the other soldiers—and naturally they found the gun. Then they really went wild and actually thought the bishop, or any member of the religious personnel, was a spy."

The Communists first placed Bishop Donaghy under house

---

[1] In 1962, Bishop Paschang was in serious condition in St. Paul's Hospital in Hong Kong. He later suffered a stroke and became paralyzed.

arrest in an attempt to starve him. But Wong Cheung Choy, a Wuchow lawyer who is now the principal of Maryknoll's Bishop Ford School in Hong Kong, smuggled food in to him at the risk of his own life.

Early one morning the bishop was taken to prison. "I saw Bishop Donaghy and Doctor Wallace [Superintendent of Stout Memorial Baptist Hospital in Wuchow] being led away just as I came out of church," Father Rielly said. "Nobody else saw or heard from him again for six months."

With Father Justin Kennedy, Bishop Donaghy shared a cell next to one occupied by Dr. Wallace. The doctor was a favorite of Maryknoll priests. Although he often irked his mission board by sending late progress reports, his heart was with the Chinese. A highly competent surgeon and a kindly man with an engaging, whimsical smile, Dr. Wallace never asked his patients for money. Even some of the Communists liked him. "Doctor Wallace is not only a good doctor, but he is a good man," said Comrade Lee, Communist political commissar of Wuchow, whose life had been saved by an operation performed by Dr. Wallace. The doctor's prison interrogation was ordered by Commissar Lee.

The physician was paraded through the freezing streets in his pajamas, then interrogated for inhuman lengths of time and accused of mass murders.

Other Maryknollers, also exhausted by interminable cross-examination, suddenly heard Dr. Wallace singing and shouting, then laughing uncontrollably. The guards told the bishop to quiet him, but he had little success. Finally Sister Rosalia, imprisoned across the corridor, tried to calm him, but his condition grew worse and one day he did not even recognize her. The next morning—February 9, 1951—his body was hanging from a rope made of torn bed sheets.

The turnkey ordered the Maryknoll priests to take down the body. While it was stiff and had obviously been without life for hours, the neck bore none of the usual marks of discoloration from strangulation.

Meanwhile, Communist armies marched into Yeungkong, and a political officer immediately posted a notice on the church door stating that all religious services were forbidden. All church property was seized and the church was converted into a rice granary. Then soldiers marched to the homes that Father Aloysius Rechsteiner maintained for the blind and orphaned and requested that everyone denounce him. Everyone remained silent. But Communist newspapers in Canton reported that "the Yeungkong group was the most obstinate."

By July 9, 1951, all Maryknoll priests had been told to leave the country and never come back. The orphaned and blind were left to their own devices.

Maryknoll's church in closeby Lukwan, where Father Edward Moffett was pastor, was used as a meeting hall and torture chamber. Father Moffett's catechist was hanged by his thighs until he "confessed," then was immediately executed for his "crime." Later the priest learned from escapees that so many landlords and accused criminals were beaten insensible and dragged around the chapel that the entire floor and lower parts of the walls were red with blood.

The Communists went to great extremes on Father Bob Greene, pastor of six small valley villages in the Kweilin diocese at Tungan. He had remained with his people during the Japanese war and was respected for it.

A stocky Communist major settled everything the first day he arrived, in April 1951. Father Greene was placed under house arrest and charged with being an American spy. His assistants—Fathers Irwin D. Nugent and Gregory J. Gilmartin—were ordered out as "not wanted." Chinese Sisters and catechists were returned to their native villages.

The Communists' second act was to hang the peaceful-looking picture of Mao Tse-tung over the church altar and paint symbols for "freedom of religion" on the outside walls. Soldiers ordered the worshipers away with bayonets, then filled the church with mud and spittle and sealed the door with bricks.

When Father Greene protested, the officer replied, with a straight face, "The People's government allows everyone to practice religion as he wishes, but assembly is not allowed."

Father Greene's guard, a young country boy, advised the priest to "confess everything."

"I'm not guilty of any crime against the government," the priest replied.

"Everyone is guilty until he confesses and repents," the soldier said. "Mao Tse-tung is our savior and is all-merciful. Confess, and everything will be all right."

The boy was sincere. The Communists had slavishly copied the Catholic Church's organization. Lenin was God. Mao Tse-tung was the Savior, his politburo the Twelve Apostles, and their disciples were inflamed with all the zeal of early Christians. Even the Communist major insisted that the Apostles and their followers had lived in a state of pure Communism. He omitted the promise of eternal reward.

Later the priest witnessed Communists beneath his window confessing their "sins" in open meetings. They admitted to such faults as "weeping at reactionary father's execution," and like the Catholics, gave themselves penances of fasting. If their leader thought their penances too light, he invoked sterner measures.

When Father Greene asked an officer why he worked the people so hard, the man replied, "For the greater glory of the Party." And the priest remembered telling the people to work "for the greater glory of God."

Father Greene had preached redemption through the Cross by sacrifice. The Communists in Tungan now told the people they could be redeemed through the Party by sacrifice.

Father Greene was allowed to walk to the market place, where one or two people whispered furtively that they had been ordered not to speak to him. Then he was locked in his chapel and for weeks lived solely on eggs from his few chickens.

The priest stared out his window for hours. He could see little children foregoing their traditional games to play "mock trial." A victim would be dragged forth, denounced, then "executed." Older children participated in the Yangko, a snake dance carried out by drums and signifying a Communist victory. There had been no folk dances in China's old morality, but now boys and girls danced in the streets during the executions of landlords and intellectuals. Most of these youngsters were his parishioners' children. When the children joined the newly formed Youth Corps, they repeatedly denounced their parents and their pastor.

Next came the Judases. They told Father Greene that they were witnesses to the faith of Communism, just as the early Christians testified to their own creed. The leader was Leang Fan, a schoolteacher and one of Father Greene's good friends. A few minutes later a squad of soldiers burst into the rectory, looking for hidden guns. And they had the evidence. Leang, who had been an undercover Communist lieutenant for years, swore that Father Greene had a cache of arms on the premises. Another man, who had delivered many articles for Father Greene, said the priest had been a notorious guerrilla chieftain and had armed his men.

Father Greene's trial began on Palm Sunday. The first witness was Ah Hiu, the priest's longtime faithful cook. He testified that Father Greene had paid to have a Communist soldier murdered.

Lieutenant Leang brusquely announced that Father Greene had been found guilty and was to be shot immediately. The priest began an Act of Contrition, but the Communist laughed and walked off with his soldiers.

The Maryknoller was locked in a convent room. He was awakened nightly, placed under a white light, and questioned well into the next day. Nerves wrecked, he sometimes awoke automatically confessing to a long list of crimes he knew nothing about.

The adjoining convent room was now used as an interrogation and torture parlor. Father Greene, who had hidden his Mass kit, could hear the Reds questioning a Chinese Sister. He took heart when he heard her tiny, angry voice rising above the interrogators, denying the charges against her pastor. Nothing—not even threatening her family or own life—broke her. She finally was led away and never heard from again, but that one small courageous voice fed the spark that kept the almost unbalanced priest from opening an artery in his wrist with a safety pin.

Then a judge and official Communist photographer arrived with some startling evidence against the priest. They had a picture of Father Greene, taken months before, on which they had superimposed a toy medal, given Father Greene by a young relative. The photo, the judge exclaimed, was proof enough. The priest was an American spy.

Father Greene was allowed only three hours of sleep every other night during the week-long trial. If he attempted to correct any of the false witnesses, he was silenced with a rifle butt. On Easter Sunday the mob shouted for the priest's death. When the judge asked what should be done with him, there was a roar like that which must have come from Jerusalem:

"*Sha!*" ("Kill!")

The crowd was allowed to hit Father Greene with stones and filth.

The judge pronounced the sentence—death by beheading. Then, in a low voice, he said, "*Wan liao* [It is finished]."

But—again following the reasoning of the inadvisability of creating foreign martyrs—Father Greene was put on a Kwelin bus with a squad of soldiers the next morning, then pulled off at every little town along the way and exhibited as "an American spy." He was put on a train to Canton, finally arriving at the Lowu border bridge. He was left alone on the Communist end, and when he saw a man on the British side nod, he stumbled ahead and began walking in circles.

# 17.

## THE PIONEERS

**T**WO unusual young men arrived in the same China district bordering Hong Kong in 1925. One was a Maryknoll priest, the other a Chinese Communist intellectual. Each was killed by the followers of the other, but what happened between them became a shadow play between Catholicism and Communism in China.

When Francis X. Ford of Maryknoll settled in Kaying, he almost had to use pagans as altar boys. He found six Catholics in his parish, and no one else would speak to him. His province was one of the most backward in China, and Father Ford was a foreigner among several million pagans.

His adversary was Peng Pai, who had fled his home town of Haifeng, less than a hundred miles from Kaying, after an unsuccessful uprising in Canton. Moreover, Peng had been a rich landlord who had given his land to the peasants there. If ignorant people in Kwangtung province were distrustful of outsiders, they saw a brother in Peng Pai.

Father Ford learned that many farmers turned to banditry because they were always in debt to the loan sharks. He initiated a farming program to free the farmer and raise the local standard of living. The Haifeng Reds sneered that he would have to shoot the landlords to accomplish these aims, but backed by rice banks and credit unions, Father Ford's plan was an immediate success. He founded schools while the Communists whispered that he was "trying to buy the hearts of the Chinese people." But despite being a foreigner and the butt of Communist slander, the priest became a father image in Kaying.

In 1926, a Communist gang from Haifeng stoned Father Ford's Siaolok mission. For the next twenty-five years they harassed Maryknoll missions, threatening the catechists and terrorizing the farmers. A 1929 Maryknoll bulletin reported: "Reds have taken over Chungyou, one of the Kaying outstations. Annual Kaying retreat postponed until situation becomes stabilized." When the Communists attacked the village and wrecked his chapel, Father Patrick Malone—one of Father Ford's assistants—dressed himself as a Chinese and escaped from the mob.

The survivors of the renegade training regiment that sparked the Canton revolt followed Peng Pai to Haifeng and there established the first Communist society in China—the Hailufeng Soviet. The town of Haifeng was called Little

Moscow. The refugees now disguised themselves as the First Division of the Chinese Workers' and Peasants' Union, later known as the Communist Farmers' Union. Several of the men who came to Haifeng in 1925 are now high government officials in Red China.

Caught in the middle, landlords were not fond of either Peng Pai or Father Ford.

Father Ford's objective was to build a road of social justice to Christianity. To accomplish this, he developed a working philosophy and a guide to social action illustrated by his farming cooperatives and schools.

Peng Pai, now chairman of the new Farmers' Union, told his followers that the Communist aim was to destroy the landlords by force, and encouraged the farmers to turn to banditry and terrorism, crying, "We thirst for the last drop of the enemy's blood!"

Peng became a martyr to the Communist cause [1] the same year Father Ford was consecrated Bishop of Kaying. He chose one word for the motto on his Episcopal shield: *Condolere* (Compassion). To suffer *with*—not just *for*.

In 1950, when Bishop Ford's seminary and convent were still growing, the Red Farmers' Union reported to Peking that he was raising "a black army" to resist Communism. For once they were right.

From the pattern of events that followed, it seems a safe conjecture that Mao Tse-tung and the old Haifeng Reds had

---

[1] Peng Pai was captured and executed by Chiang Kai-shek's troops in Shanghai in 1929.

made Bishop Ford their number one religious target in South China. The bishop's social program was widespread.

Before the Communists came to Kaying, Bishop Ford had considered building a cathedral. In December 1950, however, the Communists froze all American property in China and began expelling religious personnel. Within the next year 210 Maryknollers were jailed or expelled.

Two days before Christmas 1950, Communist soldiers smashed in the door of Bishop Ford's rectory, looking for "several criminal landlords in hiding." They locked the bishop in his room, and from that day forward no priest had an opportunity to speak to him.

Five Maryknoll Sisters were confined in the cellar of their convent and the entire compound was placed under military guard.

The bishop's house was now lighted day and night as professional Communist teams searched his files for "spy evidence." They were building an elaborate case against Bishop Ford in order to destroy the popular image. There was room for only one father image in China—Mao Tse-tung. They were careful, however, to limit their charges to the political and not the religious.

Bishop Ford had kept a complete correspondence file during his twenty-five years in Kaying, and the Communists evidently knew it. Letters between him and the American Consul at Swatow were printed, detective-story fashion, in the Canton newspapers. The consul had warned the bishop that he was in danger from the Communists, and nearly every letter contained some reference to Communism.

One of the bishop's letters was a copy of a 1948 reply to Governor T. V. Soong, Chiang Kai-shek's brother-in-law. The governor had written Bishop Ford asking for his counsel on how to improve economic conditions in the area and how to combat the steady growth of Communism.

The Red commissar in Kaying charged the bishop with being "a Koumintang agent" and "a spy for the United States." Catholics in the territory were subjected to terror, but notwithstanding Red threats upon their lives, more than 1,000 Kaying Chinese signed a petition for the release of Bishop Ford. Many of these Catholics were taken "for questioning" and never heard of again.

Sister Joan-Marie, the bishop's secretary, underwent a special grilling. She knew that the Communists were now building a great propaganda campaign against him and that "he had become pale, haggard and gaunt." The Canton newspaper accounts of the charges against Bishop Ford were reprinted in Moscow. Professsional interrogation teams questioned him daily in five-hour sessions.

On the morning of April 14, 1951, Bishop Ford and Sister Joan-Marie were taken to court, with bound hands, to hear their sentences. They had already been tried *in absentia*. But the Kaying judge reneged and said they were being sent to the provisional prison at Canton to be sentenced by the delegates of the Communist Party.

The Reds tied Bishop Ford and Sister Joan-Marie in the same manner that they had bound Bishop Paschang. With his hands behind him, the bishop was forced to carry his bedding, a heavy bundle tied with bamboo strips that lacerated his fingers. The two "imperialist spies" were paraded to the bus station while the crowds, whipped up by Communist agents, cursed at them.

At Hingning, the next day, the Maryknollers were forced to walk from the bus stop outside of town to the jail, still carrying their baggage. Middle-school students, rehearsed by Party workers, lined the road. They were armed with stones, clubs and garbage, but the bishop stalked slowly and deliberately between the lines, looking neither left nor right. One of the students walking in front of Bishop Ford carried a banner which read: THE PEOPLE'S GOVERNMENT WELCOMES THE SPY FORD.

The bloodlust of the crowd rose mercurially and it began beating even the thirty escorting soldiers. They scuttled to safety, leaving their charges in the hands of the screaming students.

At least three times on that passsage through the streets of Hingning, Bishop Ford was knocked to the bricks. Each time he rose painfully and slowly, but he still refused to run through the crowd. His deliberate manner infuriated the mob further. Jeers and curses rose higher and clubs swung faster. Bricks were torn from the streets for ammunition.

Sister Joan-Marie's calmness throughout the ordeal had left the Party workers frustrated. That night in Hingning Prison she was made to sit on an improvised throne while a crowd of people passed before her, calling out: "Where is your God now?"

The next day Bishop Ford and Sister Joan-Marie were on their way again. Their ropes were exchanged for heavier ones that had been soaked in water so they would bind more tightly as they dried. The Communists now tied the bishop's ropes in such a way that from a hole cut in the back of his padded gown one end hung down to look like a monkey's tail. It was another humiliating device, but it did not break the bishop's icy calm.

At three other towns Bishop Ford and Sister Joan-Marie were beaten and forced to go through the same performance. The tour finally ended at the big prison on Yellow Flower Road in Canton.

The Maryknollers were placed in different cell blocks of the provisional prison "for political incorrigibles," where they slept on the floor. There were no beds.

Communist indoctrination was conducted a minimum of twelve hours a day, Sister Joan-Marie later recalled in Hong Kong. "When the Communists began washing our brains," she said, "these affairs filled the prisoners with hysteria. The guards beat them while the screaming and denunciations rose."

The Communists gradually broke up friendships among the prisoners. Most were apparently of good character and education, but they turned against each other by promises, lies and threats which transformed them into creatures of suspicion, hate and deceit.

At this time the father of John Yap, the first student at Bishop Ford's seminary, walked from Kaying to the Canton prison to plead for the bishop's life. Despite the great risk to his own life, he tried for days to talk to the Communist officials in the city, but they refused to see him.

Sister Joan-Marie caught several glimpses of the bishop during January, 1952. Once she saw him plainly through a hole in the prison gate. His right arm was linked in the arm of another prisoner, and he had a cane in his left hand. He was walking with great difficulty, taking very small steps. "I got a good view of his face," she said. "He was emaciated and weak, and looked like an old man of a hundred years. He had a beard that was like white cotton. His hair was long and white."

Her next glimpse of Bishop Ford was when he was carried out to the prison yard over a peasant's shoulder, like a sack.

On August 16, 1952, Sister Joan-Marie was told by prison officials that Bishop Ford was dead. "Old age" was given as the reason, and she was shown six photographs purportedly taken of the bishop on his deathbed. One showed him in a bed, with a doctor and a nurse at his side. His head was swathed in bandages.

The warden told Sister Joan-Marie that the bishop had died on February 21, and they gave her a testimonial to sign saying that his death was due to "illness and old age, despite the medical care given him."

Sister Joan-Marie knew better. Like the landlords of Shumkai, Bishop Ford had been deliberately starved to death, perhaps on the same daily ration of rice—two ounces.

T'song K'i Yao, the police chief who directed the interrogation of Bishop Ford, knew the prelate well. A month after Bishop Ford's death, T'song entered the bishop's former cell and hanged himself.

At this time Father Mark Tennien arrived at Maryknoll House in Hong Kong with detailed reports on Chinese Communist techniques and tactics. The Communists had made the mistake of allowing Father Tennien to observe their program for fifteen months. In Shumkai, or Blue Cloud County, in Maryknoll's Wuchow diocese, Father Tennien saw how the Communists mismanaged the economy and switched from mass murder to brainwashing.

In November 1950, as Chinese Communists crossed the Yalu River into Korea, Red cadres began to instigate a reign of terror "among all reactionaries." But entire villages sent their elders to Father Tennien, asking for baptism, while Communist agents were unable to convert a single village to Communist doctrine. The event was made into the American movie, *Miracle of Blue Cloud County*.

There was only one way to stop the mission. Soldiers burst into Father Tennien's rectory and searched for "hidden guns" and locked the pastor in his room. The priest was confronted by "witnesses" who had been former teachers at his Sacred Heart School. They were Communist agents.

Familiar with Communist patterns the pastor of Blue Cloud had hidden his house keys in his room, and now "burglarized" his own stores of canned goods at night. When he ran short, boys brought food to his window. The Reds, who had hoped to starve him into a confession and a plea for an exit permit, were puzzled as the foreigner gained weight.

Professional interrogators grilled the pastor daily until his nerves were raw and he would jump at a word or knock. His nights were sleepless as the Reds arrived at all hours with petty demands. One priest in the district, recalled Father Tennien, begged to be jailed to be rid of the pressure.

For fifteen months Father Tennien watched the Communists shoot landlords, then turn to slowly starving them to death on a daily ration of two ounces of rice for each man. Approximately 3,000 landlords of Blue Cloud County died in this manner. The priest saw the land-reform teams divide the landlords' holdings among the peasants. He also saw that they were distributing poverty, not wealth.

It was true that landlords had kept many Chinese farmers in hopeless debt by hoarding rice whenever the crops failed in order to lend one bushel for two at the next harvest. But now that the landlords were dead or gone and the poor owned all the land, they discovered that they were worse off than before.

"The peasant was now taxed two hundred percent higher than before in order to feed the Red army," he explained, "and the new horde of officials. Ten times more than under the Nationalists."

The Chinese elders began shuffling about Blue Cloud, muttering, "It is their world now." (An ancient expression used in China whenever tyrants come to power.) To dispel the gloom of the farmers over the new taxes, Party workers kept the people keyed up with a continual round of parades, speeches, meetings, firecracker displays and executions.

Within two months, Father Tennien observed, the Communists had liquidated every influential person in Blue Cloud, except those who had fled to Hong Kong. All education and leadership of the old regime was eradicated, and hard money disappeared.

Father Tennien was placed in a local jail on March 20, 1951, charged with threatening to kill a soldier. There were 500 other prisoners, many of whom had not had a bath in months and had developed skin diseases. The stench was overpowering. A cellmate taught Father Tennien how to "pop" lice with a thumbnail. All twelve cell blocks were given five minutes each morning and night for toilet call in the pigpen. Each prisoner got a cup of water which had been used for washing rice and 3 cents' worth of vegetables daily.

The prisoners were indoctrinated at long, noisy sessions. America was called the Paper Tiger, and all Americans were "weak, soft and decadent." The exploitation of China by the foreigner was dwelt upon, and the story of Mao Tse-tung was repeated endlessly.

The highlight of the daily indoctrination meeting was the singing contest among the prisoners. Each cell block vied with the others in shouting Communist songs, and since Father Tennien liked to sing, he led his own cell block to victory and the applause of the other prisoners. The Communist officials were infuriated, recognizing the subtle irony of the American priest, an incorrigible Red-baiter, leading a program of Communist propaganda. They laid plans for him.

When the Communists came to Blue Cloud, they no longer skinned men alive or crucified them. "At first," said Father Tennien, "the Commmunists simply beat prisoners to death. Millions were executed before they tried brainwashing. For awhile a thousand a day committed suicide in Shanghai, according to mission reports, rather than face the new 'questioning.' In Blue Cloud, my own most outstanding parish family committed suicide after two years of unremitting mental torture."

Ex-soldiers, intellectuals and landlords had been doomed from the start, and the blankets of the executed prisoners were piled outside Father Tennien's cell window to be claimed by relatives. One day the missioner counted more than 150 blankets in one stack. His cellmates insisted that the Reds were now shooting 10 to 15 "incorrigible reactionaries" a day in that one jail.

Then an interrogation team began tackling Father Tennien by alternating between winsome smiles and promises of more food and a shorter sentence to masks of hatred and threats of torture and execution.

Some of the Blue Cloud prisoners broke under such psychological warfare. "*Fei hwa* [The words of a mad dog]," said the others. The unbalanced ones, some of them Father Tennien's own parishioners, now heard voices accusing them, and there were screams and weeping in the night. Finally the *Fei hwa* people were shot.

After two months of "questioning," the warden put Father Tennien in solitary confinement for his stubbornness in refusing to sign a confession that he had threatened to kill a soldier. A month later the Communists deleted the word "kill," and the priest finally signed. He received an exit permit and was escorted out of the country.

Monsignor Romaniello and Father Edwin McCabe were at Kweilin when the Communists arrived. When the commissar barged in, he found the monsignor calmly reading *The Last Stand*, a book about a Communist threat of many years ago.

At first the Party workers tried to bait Monsignor Romaniello into a trap of semantics, but he was no timid soul and he was an authority on Marxist-Leninist dialectics. In fluent Chinese, he challenged the commissar to a public debate. The official retired to think it over, then replied by handing the monsignor his exit permit.

Monsignor Romaniello was allowed a last Mass in his church. After Mass was over, his altar boy Su Lo extinguished the altar candles, then brought out a ladder and placed it under the sanctuary lamp. As he watched the boy, the priest recalled lighting the lamp the day the church had been consecrated.

Su Lo opened the ladder slowly. Of all the people in the church only he had understood the full significance of the coming of the Reds. Ascending the ladder deliberately, as though it were part of the Mass, Su Lo bent over and blew out the candle in the sanctuary lamp—the lamp that is never allowed to go out while the church is functioning.

Monsignor Romaniello and the people stood still. As Su Lo replaced the red glass chimney, the monsignor saw a wisp of smoke curl upward.

The Catholic Church was in silence in China.

# 18.

## THE SECRET DIARY

**T**HERE is only one Maryknoll missionary, Bishop James E. Walsh, in China today. He refused a proffered exit permit and is serving a twenty-year sentence in Shanghai's Ward Road prison as "an enemy of the People."

Maryknoll does not have contact with Bishop Walsh, and there is little valid information trickling out of Red China. What is happening in the vast silence sealed off behind Hong Kong is a major mystery in the Free World today.

Maryknoll, which is training personnel to return to China should the Communists ever lose power, is not ignorant about present-day conditions in China and around its former missions there. It saw to that when it trained Chinese priests like Father Aloysius Ao, a courageous little man from Malaya.

Maryknoll priests in Hong Kong were prepared for a rebuttal when the Chinese Communist government announced, on July 12, 1962, that limited freedom of religion had been granted the masses. A brown envelope containing the secret diary of Father Ao had reached the Maryknoll house in Hong Kong.

Communist slander, the priest noted, touched Father Ao's parish in Hingning in January 1951, when the Reds held an all-night victory party and mock funeral for the pastor in his own church. Next day the judge read off "evidence" that Father Ao had killed a water buffalo, and the Communist-inspired crowd chanted: "Death or life in prison." The judge, however, sentenced Father Ao to only one year at hard labor. The year totaled thirty months before he was released. For the next nine years he secretly documented Communist religious persecution. Some excerpts are:

### 1953

*June 17*—Today I walked out of prison with nothing on but a pair of drawers and a sleeveless shirt. Free again after 30 months, if it is freedom. I cannot say that I'm much better off but at least it's far better than the dungeon.

Have almost forgotten how to say Mass. Both prayers and liturgy vanished from my head after one year of brainwashing. Happy to find my missal even though it is old and worn and many pages are missing.

I am now living with a friend in a small rented room, bare and empty, in a tenement house that belongs to a Catholic physician who is working for the people's government. I am allowed to stay here only three months. After that, I have to go to the authorities for extension.

Every other day I walk to the markets one and a half miles away to carry firewood, coal, charcoal, beans or any coolie work handy. I can balance about 100 pounds with a pole and make about 50 cents a trip. Not very good, ho?

*July 1*—Tension has aggravated my rectal trouble. My teeth are giving me fits, too. They kicked me in the face in prison, smashing my glasses and I can't see 20 feet without them.

*August 15*—It is The Feast of the Assumption and my people are very happy that I have returned. Just like fish returned to water. Had over 200 communions. Gave last sacraments to 10 people and had 30 baptisms. Hingning is a big territory and most of my Christians are in the villages. Almost got into trouble with the authorities for being so far afield. Held by the police for two hours and, boy, did the future look dark!

*December 25*—150 people came to midnight Mass Christmas Eve. After High Mass in the morning many people came to tea and everyone thoroughly enjoyed themselves. Held Benediction at four this afternoon. I tried to impress on them that our Church is not built just with bricks but that it rises from the hearts of those who enter it. Bricks can be levelled to the ground but the Church in our hearts can never be destroyed.

Was very happy in preparing for Christmas. Built a small

manger and hung holy pictures on the walls of my sitting room which I converted into a temporary chapel with lights, flowers, and lanterns. Can now say public Mass in my house and 40–50 people attend.

## 1954

*May 6*—Saw my catechist again. Communism has brought added difficulties to his village. Says the people have reached a stage where they no longer have the heart to think of days gone by.

*July 22*—The fruits of labor must be all sold to the State, such as rice, oil, sugar, etc. All purchasing and selling is controlled by the State. Each peasant is allowed a ration of approximately four ounces of rice a day. This is the maximum. As for sugar, if one has a doctor's prescription stating that the bearer is ill, and in addition a certificate from the local authorities, he can get permission to purchase a half ounce.

*August 2*—In Kaying the influence of the Church has all but disappeared. The Catholics do not dare let themselves be heard. The Reds have countless ways and means of persecution and it is their aim to drive Christianity out of China. But no independent Church has been started here yet!

*August 17*—Red officials are now occupying three buildings in Bishop Ford's compound. The large crucifix in the Kaying church, which was made of copper or bronze, has been hacked to pieces and sold by the soldiers. Chalices are used by soldiers for drinking tea. The people said Mass wine was sold at so much per bottle. The church itself is now a county seat. Other churches have been turned into granaries or meeting halls or jails. Even the hilltop Buddhas have been smashed.

*October 3*—Many of my friends here have been tortured and brain-washed in prison. One Christian was jailed for no other reason than that he had been friendly to Bishop Ford.

*October 10*—It was a mistake to make use of my British citizenship as a means for them to give me less annoyance. The whole thing has boomeranged. The result is that I am under a terrific mental and physical strain and in constant danger of being imprisoned again.

*October 21*—Now having rent trouble. My doctor friend who rented this house, has been transferred and demoted. The Reds are playing a dirty game. I'll now have a hard time finding another place and my communist friends will have killed two birds with one stone.

*November 1*—Conditions are now deteriorating. My milk business had gone from bad to worse. My cow died. Now back to working on the land with the peasants. Weather ruined the spring harvest and there was a drouth this fall. Rice, peanuts, potatoes, tomatoes, etc., are all below normal.

Rice is now restricted to four *hap* [1] per person per day. Farmers must sell the white rice at harvest time to the government at a fixed price. Later when they buy rice for their

---

[1] About a cupful.

own consumption they are given cheap red rice. People are now on a day to day ration basis. The monthly ration of peanut oil is four ounces. Salt is scarce and brown sugar is rationed at one ounce per month.

*November 8*—At first the communists came to Kayıng as liberators, treating the people very well and making many promises of aid and toleration. They promised protection to the Church and said they were working along material lines just as we were working along spiritual lines, so that there was room for both sides to work amicably for the welfare of the State. This attitude did not last very long.

Gradually, as they became more numerous, they began to show their true colors. Churches were banned and used as granaries or meeting halls. Then they began to work on the Chinese clergy and laity.

Everybody is still frightened, not knowing who is the next to be brought before the accusers. Fathers cannot trust their sons and vice versa. Red pressure is growing on religion and I feel that I will be arrested again and soon. Heard one priest in Canton has been handcuffed hand and foot for six months. Anything sent to him has been returned. His case is bad.

Because of my vocation I have always been *persona non grata* with the Reds, a condition greatly intensified by the false impeachment of Bishop Ford. The fact that I am an ex-convict (I feel it an honor to suffer for Christ) is another blot on my record here.

*November 11*—A fallen-away Catholic has told the authorities that I have been celebrating Mass "under the counter." They are now putting two and two together and, by gosh, will get five as usual. I shall hang on as long as possible, for I cannot leave my flock. I am scared. The strain is unbearable. I feel so oppressed that I am physically sick.

*November 13*—Am now under strict surveillance. My movements are restricted. Can't even go to Canton for dental treatment. My passport has made things worse. They've confiscated it, knocking me to the floor while screaming threats and curses. They don't recognize my British citizenship and they have taken away my rights as a Chinese citizen.

*November 19*—Every now and then I have to go around in the streets under armed guard to show the people that I am an enemy of the State. My condition is that of a semi-convict. I am not allowed to visit anyone or vice versa. My friends advise me to leave for Swatow or Canton but I cannot do that.

## 1955

*January 10*—The Agrarian Reform authorities have now given permission to let the people pray again and attend Mass in public. So the game goes. Every Sunday now I have three Masses. Christians are allowed to come and go freely. Even during the week a number of Christians attend Mass.

*February 6*—Am at my wits' end just to live. No one will give me a job and I have no money. Conditions now are different than in the beginning of Red rule. Several years ago private business and free enterprise were still going and Catholics were able to give me a hand. Now everyone has a hard time keeping alive. Having been in prison, I am now a marked man. My movements are under strict surveillance. There are no private jobs. All positions are governmental. Priests all over the territory are working where they can, in shops, raising bees, collecting resin from trees, selling herbs, farming. As for myself, I can find nothing.

*June 17*—Two years ago I walked out of prison. Can't see where I've made any progress.

*June 21*—My birthday. I am 43. June 29 will be the 12th year of my ordination. Whoever reads these lines please pray for me on these dates.

Conditions all around are about the same. My teeth are giving me lots of trouble but the Reds are worse. My friends are all in prison now. It is only a question of time until I am back again with them.

*August 29*—For the ordinary person in good standing it is difficult to get work as finding a needle in a haystack. For a priest with a prison record (and more than half in China now have one) it is a double headache.

The "pressure" of the communists on religious personnel is getting heavier. There isn't any sign of easing off and it looks that they are determined to squash the Church. Being the former pastor and member of the diocesan council here,

I am always the butt of their endless baitings, probes and indignities.

*September 9*—A Red typhoon has hit the Church in China again! It is almost as bad as the one in 1952. Yesterday they began jailing a great number (exact figure cannot be ascertained but some put it at 300) of clerics, including the Bishop of Shanghai and many of the faithful. The storm is raging very fiercely. A gigantic campaign has started to throttle and choke the Body of Christ out of China. It is merely a question of time until those clerics who have refused to join the Red Church will suffer the same fate. We live from day to day not knowing when our number will be up. My people are afraid to pray fearing that members of their own families will report them.

Without the Grace of God I would have lost my mind long ago. I know that I am not alone. The servants of God are being collared for the same old sin of not kowtowing to Caesar.

*December 3*—Today is The Feast of St. Francis Xavier, patron of the missions. The black clouds are still thick and heavy. The signs are there. I shall be in prison again and so on. God be with me.

## 1956

*January 19*—Not yet in prison but how long I can keep out of it the Lord only knows. I was held by the police today while they fine-combed my room and carried off everything they thought suspicious.

I am now in restrictive custody. Half-free, half-convict. Have great difficulty in getting flour for altar breads and wine for Mass.

Things are getting worse now. People have stopped coming to my house for Mass. They are too scared. My old church here is now being used as a branch of the Nengchung Middle School.

*June 25*—Many Christians are being jailed now. Was taken to Swatow for two weeks of brain-washing.

*July 20*—Still under restrictive custody. What this phrase means! I offer all my tribulations, sufferings and ignominy to Christ. In Swatow they asked me how many Catholics were in Hingning and the economic status of the Church there.

*September 3*—A very small section of the clergy has joined the Anti-Imperialist and Patriotic Society. I'd rather let them have my head than jot down my name on this list.

*September 23*—I can now leave the house but not beyond the city limits. The town of Hingning isn't very big. A very few Catholics slip in to see me. My cracked dental plate makes it difficult for me to eat and I cannot see without my glasses. My flock is in bad shape all around, too, spiritually and temporally.

Rain is badly needed. For my part, I pray more for the rain of heavenly graces.

## 1957

*March 21*—Now we are in the season of Lent but the Reds have eased off a bit although I am still restricted. About 40 came to Mass in my room. I say Mass on the table without altar cloths or vestments. The people kneel on the floor. Two Chinese Sisters left the community and got married. Nearly all the Sisters have worked in the labor communes.

*April 23*—Had more than 100 for Easter Masses (two). This number is small compared to former days but I'm satisfied. The majority are still too scared to even approach a priest. We are still under attack in the press and in books.

One false move and I'll be looking through bars. But when the situation improves again I plan to go into the villages to look for my flock. Before, I did so stealthily but in the future—if I have the chance—I am going to do it openly!

*May 15*—Need lots of things to have this black hole of a room decently fixed but figure it's better to go slow and carefully. Some people think things have changed for the better but it's difficult to forget what happened several years ago, or to be blind to the forces at work here.

The Patriotic Society will be formed here this month to boost the Red Church. The slogan is Love the Country, Love the Church!

My restrictive custody has eased off a bit. It's a game with the Reds. I can now get into the countryside for sick calls and visitations. The flock has braced up a bit but most are still scared. Hingning is a vast territory and I need a bicycle but the cost of even a second-hand one is out of sight. I have almost forgotten the taste of coffee, butter, chocolate and other delicacies.

*May 29*—They've taken me to Swatow again. The brain-washing comes up in 20 days or so. The Reds are determined to have an independent church started by apostate priests. They use thousands of tricks. Been here a month now. Then on to Canton for more indoctrination. A friend helped me get some glasses in Swatow but they don't fit. Something wrong with the left lens.

### 1958

*February 6*—In Swatow again. Scheduled to go to Canton at the end of this month. Have been holding the fort for more than a month now. The pressure is so great that I will have to give in on some things, i.e., to articles not against faith and morals. Am still allowed to recognize the Holy Father as head of the Church and vicar of Christ. This I cannot give away at any price. Saw another priest today whom I knew had suffered heavily under brain-washing and asked him if he was still with us. He said, "Before God's Face I am faithful to our honored bishop!"

Told I must attend the Catholic clergy's conferences April 12 in Canton. Will be the same old thing all over. It is rumored the conference will last two months. From now on I will be more closely watched.

*March 12*—Just got back from Swatow. Not giving me much time to myself these days.

*April 9*—Canton. They are a smart lot these communists. They are playing one man against another here to destroy the unity of the Church, but only a few have fallen for this trick. Nevertheless, the Church in China will be in very great difficulties quite soon. Will be here a month.

*April 16*—Just got rid of an attack of the flu, but the aftermath hangs on like a leech. But there are no good real doctors in Canton. Most of them have been tranferred up north or have been swallowed up by the various departments.

*April 27*—The Reds made us all sign a paper that we would not ask any foreign missions for aid. Penalty will be a big stretch in prison or labor camp. They mean it, too, as they are determined to break up all relations with the universal Church. They are even suspicious of the letters from my family in Malaya. Only a question of time.

### 1960

*April 2*—Chinghai prison. We are in the far north and in mountainous country. The border weather is cold and snow often falls in the spring. I now have tuberculosis and beri-beri. Getting weak. Over 10,000 prisoners are working here. It is a place for "political incorrigibles." The work is to dig coal. It is very hard. Every day we must work 10 hours. No rest, no Sunday. Only a bit of rice and a little vegetables twice a day. No meat. No food to buy. Two ounces of rice a day is slow starvation. Because of the labor and hunger my body becomes thin and weaker day by day. They make us carry 80 to 90 catties[2] of coal 20 miles from the mine. My health is now very bad.

I cannot write more and my heart is aching. I offer everything to God and rely on His Holy Will.

Here the diary ends. Father Aloysius Ao, aged forty-eight, died November 23, 1960, in Chinghai Prison, a hard-labor camp bordering the Gobi Desert.

Maryknoll was in China for thirty-two years, but the story of Father Ao is one measure of its work there. No native priest trained by Maryknoll is known to have defected to the Communist Church.

The voice from the grave has warned that—unknown to the free world—Communist security police have been playing a deadly game with the scattered, tiny pockets of Christians in China. At least four times since 1949, according to the Ao diary, the Communists have used the promise of "freedom of religion" as a decoy to count Christians for the next bloody pogrom. Communist spies penetrate every village, and Chinese newspapers boast that half the native clergy is either dead or in prison. The rest have vanished into shops or farms as the Red Pendulum swung for a decade between "freedom of religion" and all-out terror.

Father Ao lies in an unmarked grave. The Communists made few public martyrs after 1950, and there is evidence

[2] About 120 pounds.

that they are wiping out all physical reminders of those few.

Not long ago a Kaying refugee arrived in Hong Kong. He told a Maryknoll priest that he had recently made a pilgrimage to Bishop Ford's grave. He knew the site, but was unable to find it; the field had been planted in crops.

# 19.

## THE PILOT MODEL

THE Maryknoll social idea is simply a new look at Christian charity. That and American efficiency in achievement.

In Maryknoll areas today—from Hong Kong to Peru— where most people go to bed hungry every night, a handful of men and women have helped to arrest Communism and caused Christian life to bud. Maryknoll's work is sufficiently phenomenal, in a period more noted for fact-finding surveys and crash programs, to draw a nod of approval from the conservative British press in Hong Kong and warm praise from the United States Embassy in Lima, Peru.

The Hong Kong experiment was not, however, entirely original, being but a distillation of its significant China successes. Maryknoll priests, who merely added new techniques to build the mission in Hong Kong, point out that members from the society's founders down contributed to the Hong Kong plan.

In a day when many China missioners were bemused with their own social status, Maryknoll's first departure group ate red rice "with rocks in it," slept on native *kangs* (stove beds) and scratched lice in huts of their new parishioners in order to feel *with* their people, not just *for* them. Three decades later Father Trube never thought twice about becoming the first squatter priest in the rarefied social atmosphere of the Crown colony of Hong Kong.

Bishop Ford's cooperatives preceded Father Dempsey's weaving project by more than thirty years, and Father Edmonds' effective pattern of work with juvenile delinquents in Hong Kong derived from Father Larry Conley's postwar Boys' Town in Toishan after World War II.

Chinese children who studied at Yeungkong, Maryknoll's first mission, were grown when Father Rielly and the Maryknoll Sisters planned their educational plants in Hong Kong, and even Monsignor Romaniello's idea of making noodles from U. S. surplus foods may have stemmed from a reverse attitude: Bishop James E. Walsh's constant experiments in converting Chinese food into something corresponding to the American concept of ham and eggs.

Maryknoll seminaries study the Hong Kong experiment perhaps more as an example of flexibility and adaptability than as a pilot model for the society's mission. Nonetheless, the Hong Kong team provided the initiative for ambitious programs in Latin America. These programs include low-

229

cost housing, farming and industrial cooperatives, credit unions, and improved techniques for the handling and distribution of relief supplies.

The Chinese Communists cut Maryknoll's overseas missions almost in half when they expelled religious personnel from China in the early nineteen-fifties. All the early Maryknollers were assigned to work in the Orient. Even its headquarters buildings at Ossining, New York, are of Oriental architecture. The loss of China and the threat of Communism to the entire world inspired the society to overhaul old mission techniques and develop new ones to meet a rapidly shifting situation. In this, its strategy and objective were not merely to fight Communism but first to build a temporary halfway house where the downtrodden and oppressed could adjust to the twentieth century.

In Hong Kong, Maryknollers learned how to build low-cost cottages, to get a man a job, to start him in business, to provide medical care and even to turn U. S. surplus food into native fare. It was Operation Bootstrap all the way. But most of all they learned how to give and still let a man keep his dignity; how to solidify the family, the keystone of any society, on Christian socioeconomic principles. As for themselves, they gained a new definition of teamwork and learned how to cut red tape and get an operation off the ground with dispatch and efficiency.

In Latin America, Maryknoll fanned out through the *corralónes* of Lima and Santiago, into Bolivia's jungles and the altiplano of the Andean Mountains, to apply the basic techniques of the Hong Kong experiment and add a few of its own. It found the Communists had got there first, firmly believing that history is on their side.

"It is one minute to midnight south of the border," warns Teodoro Moscoso, Administrator for the Alliance for Progress program. Half the people of Latin America are illiterate, live in squalor, and never see as much as $200 a year. Nearly all of the best land is owned by a few hundred families. There is almost no middle class. Although the majority of the peasants claim to be Catholic, their Church membership is largely nominal, and priests are few and far between. Church authorities estimate that it will take twenty years to raise up a native clergy, but some veteran missioners maintain that the Communists may be in control before then unless a revolutionary socioeconomic program is put into effect at once. Communist propaganda is aggressive, as Adlai Stevenson and Richard Nixon learned when traveling through these countries, and even the Chinese Reds are exchanging students with some of the leading universities of Latin America.

Buttressed by the Hong Kong experiment, Maryknoll's teams mounted an offensive in Peru to provide decent homes, sufficient clothing, and proper food for the Indians. Nothing stabilizes the family like home and business or farm ownership. When Maryknoll's Father Daniel B. McLellan found the Indians in the Puno region living in extreme poverty, he immediately formed a credit union and farming cooperative. Bankers in Lima said it couldn't be done, but today Maryknoll has 79 credit unions operating in Peru and has loaned more than $1 million at one-percent interest. The loss has been one ninth of one percent. Three arts and crafts schools were inaugurated and a model housing cooperative was begun. Today the Maryknoll team is working closely with the government on a plan to establish other housing cooperatives to replace other pockets of poverty.

In the recent teachers' strike in Lima, salaries were halted by the government. The Communists tried to capitalize on the situation, but a crisis was averted when the Maryknoll credit union there tided the teachers over until work was resumed.

Someone in the United States sent a tiny transistor radio to a Maryknoll priest in Peru. Priests are so scarce in Latin America that this seemed a good way to reach the people. The Maryknoll team drafted a plan for a nationwide radio network of small, inexpensive transistor sets to reduce illiteracy (Bishop James A. Walsh had always insisted that mass communications media be an integral part of the society's social program), and today there are hundreds of Maryknoll radio schools throughout the Andean Mountains of Bolivia and Peru. They help to teach the Indians Spanish, parliamentary procedure (half the Indian population does not vote), public speaking, civics with an anti-Communist slant, sanitation, hygiene and first aid.

The importance of the Maryknoll radio network is heightened by the growing aggressiveness and volume of the Peking and Moscow broadcasts to Latin America. The quality of the Voice of America is good, but the Communists broadcast 74 hours of Spanish programs weekly and 28 hours in Portuguese, the official language of Brazil. The Voice of

America cannot compete with such volume on its present budget and has no programs in Portuguese. In the Puno region the Communist radio had proved more effective than the American effort in capturing the minds of the people until the Maryknoll radio network blunted its arguments, particularly by moving native catechists into the villages to back up its broadcasts.

Bishop John W. Comber, Maryknoll's superior-general, says: "It is our objective to build the church of native stone." To help offset the country's acute shortage of priests, Maryknoll missioners have launched a drive for 2,000 catechists. It is fundamental missiology that no foreigner can displace the empathy that lies between one native and another. For this reason a good catechist can sell the ideals of the Americans to his people better than an American can, and Maryknoll claims that a catechist is the real St. Paul of the missions, entering strange villages, making friends, curing the sick, explaining away prejudices and weeding out superstitions.

Maryknoll now has 50,000 students enrolled in its mission schools, and its highly trained catechists have enabled it to rally thousands of Indians upon short notice—a technique which has already hindered Communist-hatched plots.

The Maryknoll idea in Peru calls for the establishment of an industrial or farming cooperative and a community center in each parish, with a tiny transistor radio set in every outlying village to supplement the work of the catechists.

Recognizing the effectiveness of the Maryknoll teams in raising the economic and social level of the Peruvian Indian, the United States Embassy in Lima, in an official report to Washington, said:

"Their work is a study in applied Christianity . . . Maryknoll is cutting the red tape and doing something. May God and the United States of America bless them."

Yeungkong, China, and El Salvador—Maryknoll's first and newest missions—are half a world and forty-four years apart. But the chain reaction of any mission's success, whether it be a new twist in cooperatives or an ingenious way of reaching people in remote areas, continues to lift all of Maryknoll's missions to the next higher plateau in the science of Christian humanism. The strategy is always the same; the tactics vary with the situation and locale.

Every Maryknoll camp is a sounding board for ideas. No matter how seemingly farfetched it may be, every man tosses a theory into the pot. Now and then one is raked out and considered. If the idea materializes, a Maryknoll priest gets the go signal and begins probing for a likely location. When he finds one—and he usually does—Maryknoll sends in a team to make the breakthrough. Other Maryknollers follow to widen the breach and consolidate their position. On their flanks are the Communists.

The Maryknoll plan began with its founders. The first Bishop Walsh—James Anthony—who, along with Father Thomas F. Price, founded Maryknoll, told his boys that: "It is the precious gift of initiative that marks the apostle, and every mission needs it if it is to accelerate its march beyond the humdrum rate of advance that any set of good men will maintain anywhere." He continually exhorted them to "keep eternally devising." This was in 1912, when old China missioners were stressing patience as the missioner's prime virtue. Maryknoll's first chiefs saw it differently. They advised their charges to "go slowly but go forward."

The second Bishop Walsh—James E. (no relation to the founder)—continued the pace shortly before World War II and wrote that missioner's classic, "The Kongmoon Manual." Later his "Blueprint of a Missioner" and "The Spiritual Directory of Maryknoll" were to guide thousands of Maryknoll priests. Walking in the footsteps of his predecessors, Bishop James E. Walsh proved to be another apostle of experiment and change. He was forever tinkering with new methods of attack, adopting the successful, abandoning the failures, and refusing to accept the notion prevalent in religious circles at that time that all there was to be learned about missionary work had been learned, which may be one reason why the words "expert" and "old pro" are seldom heard in Maryknoll seminaries.

As one seminary professor put it, "The Maryknoller is, more often than not, a character."

All Maryknollers seem to be the same rugged fellow with an easy grin and the callouses of hard work, but no two of them wear their hats at quite the same angle. They may brashly invite Hollywood to make movies about them, or just read letters from home to their mules, but they are team men and know how to provide an existence worthy of human dignity to thousands of desperate people.

A Hollywood director could make one of those fun-in-the-parish pictures in any Maryknoll seminary, and a sociologist could be pardoned for thinking he had discovered a pocket of original American pioneer spirit in any Maryknoll mission, but the chances are that neither would go very far toward explaining the Maryknoll Father and his job.

The Maryknoll screening committee makes every effort to weed out introverts, poor conversationalists, and those who stood in the bottom half of their class, and of course the physically unfit and emotionally unstable.

The Maryknoller is usually pragmatic, a well-adjusted fellow who likes people; the kind who can live in a piano crate and walk thirty miles a day with a pack on his back and like it. He swims, golfs, fishes and hunts. His education takes twelve years, even includes anthropology, and enables him to speak several languages, organize a cooperative, set a broken leg, operate a 1000-watt transmitter, and serve in a United Nations' agency. He learns the intricacies of writing a television script for a Tokyo audience or how to foil the machinations of a witch doctor in Guatemala or a Communist plot in Hong Kong.

At the Maryknoll Father's side is the Maryknoll Brother. The Brothers are expert carpenters, electricians, plumbers, mechanics, cooks, engineers, architects, farmers, bookkeepers, gardeners, printers, artists and teachers. It goes without saying that they take much of the load off the shoulders of their priests. Bishop James E. Walsh said of them: "Either mission work makes men resourceful, or else God picks men of resources and sends them into mission work."

Some Maryknoll Brothers have attained considerable eminence in their work.

Cardinal Cushing once praised the Maryknoll Brothers, remarking that "ninety percent of the work done that an archbishop does, a well-trained Brother could do." Unimpressed, a Maryknoll Brother replied, "Ninety percent of the work that a Brother does, a well-trained archbishop could do."

"Priests make converts, but the Sisters make Catholics." The old saying is almost true. Maryknoll Sisters' doctor-teacher teams today are traveling by muleback in Latin America—sometimes into Andean Mountains a full mile higher than the Swiss Alps—to reach the sick, the ignorant, the poor.

The classic quality of a Maryknoller is adaptability and initiative. Without either, the missioner becomes a recluse. Bishop James E. Walsh scorned mediocrity, warning: "To merely become a missioner is, of course, a superlatively easy thing. All that is required is to cross the ocean, buy a dictionary, and get to work (not necessarily too hard). Some add a typewriter and a camera; others grow a beard; still others learn to smoke a pipe." The Maryknoller has little time to become homesick or to feel sorry for himself; he enjoys his work too much for that.

Maryknoll's Father Richard S. McGonigal toiled in Bolivia for six years. His mission territory lay along 1,500 miles of the jungle banks of the Madre de Dios River. Shortly before he died (March 8, 1957), Father McGonigal wrote home:

> In what other walk of life except that of the very rich can a man have a horse, a dog, guns and a boat, and spend money

on them because they are the tools of his trade? In what other vocation can a man have days, each one of them different, where he has to travel and meet new people? Where else can he make so many new friends and feel so loved, accepted and respected?

I am very content as a missioner because in the human sphere it lifts me out of monotonous mediocrity. There comes a point in a man's life when dreams fade away and he has to adjust himself to mediocrity. I was never a great athlete nor a great intellectual. I have no musical ability. Other men had much more brilliant minds and were much more spiritual. But here on the missions I am not ordinary. I am the only priest for a thousand miles . . . I am walking in the footsteps of St. Paul . . . bungling along in my own helpless way, but in his footsteps nonetheless . . . I am a force for moral good. Sometimes I feel like the boy with his finger in the dike, but just the fact that I am here reminds the people of the ten commandments and keeps them from returning to the law of the jungle.

In Hong Kong, Korea, Formosa, Japan, the Philippines, Hawaii, Mexico, Guatemala, El Salvador, Peru, Bolivia, Chile and Tanganyika, Africa, more than 1,000 Maryknollers are trying to keep men from returning to the law of the jungle, to implant American ideals and to help men to help themselves.

# EPILOGUE

**M**AY DAY, world Communism's 4th of July, is celebrated by brandishing weapons, threatening to bury the capitalist world, and the promise of another wonderful ten-year plan.

Peasants in Communist China wanted something simpler for their 1962 May Day—food. Especially the people telling pathetic tales of eating soup made of fish bones, stalks, roots, bark and grass. As escapees from Red China repeatedly confirm, "All would go to Hong Kong today if they could slip by the guards."

On May 1, 1962, a long-promised miracle finally occurred in China's Kwangtung province. There had been panic when factories closed and workers were sent to commune farms already desperately short of food. But a strange man

brought authoritative word to villages and hamlets that anyone could move freely without exit permits to Hong Kong.
Families put their belongings in grass sacks. Some were so
excited they left everything. When the peasants reached
the main roads, they found entire hamlets and larger groups
of people who also had heard the news.

Still, there were doubts. Why, they asked, was Mao Tse-
tung, the Communist boss, allowing this? He had always
claimed Hong Kong was vicious colonialism used as a
United States base to transmit the poison causing China's
cholera epidemics and droughts.

The downtrodden Chinese were convinced the miracle
was true when they reached the heretofore closed twenty-
mile border area. Guards who had fired into crowds and
unleashed wild dogs the week before were giving directions
like helpful attendants in American filling stations. Sentries
advised against crossing at the Shumchun-Lowu border
bridge, since the British allowed only fifty Chinese with
entrance permits to enter daily. Instead, the guards pointed
out where the fence had been cut and the river was shallow
enough to wade. Thousands slipped through to freedom.

Suddenly the Chinese were surrounded by British soldiers
in blue uniforms, and helicopters hovered overhead until
truckloads of troops with knives came toward them. The
Chinese had not been told that two weeks earlier the Hong
Kong government had publicly announced that it could not
accept any additional "illegal immigrants" from China and
future ones would be deported. They still didn't know this
inside China, and thousands continued to escape.

So the wall went up. The Hong Kong government spent a reported $97,500 for barbed wire that was rolled, military style, 10 feet high and 20 feet wide to reinforce the twisting 22-mile border separating Hong Kong's New Territories and Communist China. Unlike the Berlin Wall, this iron curtain was not to keep people inside the terror of Communism. It was to keep them out.

Uncounted thousands escaped police and melted into Hong Kong. Seventy thousand refugees did not escape, were herded into detention camps, fed, questioned, then either put into trucks or a ten-car diesel switch engine and taken back to the China border. People dropped to their knees screaming, "You're sending us back to starve! Please give us a chance!" Some fought as desperately as men going to the gallows. Many screamed, *"We'll be back";* some made seven or eight attempts. Women with babies strapped to their backs begged, "They will take our children and kill us. You are sending us back to die."

Nobody would help them. The United Nations ignored the situation. The British declined volunteer and religious help. The United States, with its vast foreign aid and Peace Corps, made headlines by announcing it would accept Chinese whose applications had been processed. This did not affect the Chinese being sent back to Communism. The free world press classified the action "one of the most atrocious acts in international history." Theories arose that Mao Tse-tung lost control and people simply were being sent to Hong Kong for food. (Sentiments were reminiscent of 1921—the struggling Russian Communist Party had misused its grain and was near starvation and collapse; the American Relief Organization sent enough food for the following two years.)

If there was a food shortage in China, then why, in the same period, did Communist boats pull beside the Hong Kong trading warehouse of Jardine-Mathieson & Company and unload rice? "Yes, we're buying lots of rice from China," said T. M. Parsons, Jardine property manager.

While many prominent persons appealed to the United States to send grain to Communist China, Monsignor Romaniello found plenty of rice and wheat for the Chinese to eat. The Maryknoll priest walked into one dingy yellow warehouse in Hong Kong and found sacks piled to the ceiling. All were marked: MADE IN THE PEOPLE'S REPUBLIC OF CHINA. Three weeks later a Havana broadcast said Cuba had purchased 24 million pounds of rice from Communist China.

The Communist refugee plot began in late April. China received a diplomatic note from Britain reporting that it would not accommodate any additional Chinese refugees in Hong Kong and all that entered without exit permits would be returned. Immediately word reached Kwangtung residents that travel restrictions had been lifted. Communist border guards were told to allow movements to Hong Kong. On May 30 the guards also received orders to stop them. They followed both orders.

The latter order was the aftermath of a meeting on May 17 between Hugh Morgan, British Chargé d'Affaires in Peiping, and several officials of the Chinese Communist Ministry of Foreign Affairs. On May 29, Morgan received a memorandum that the exodus would cease. The same guards who gave directions to escapees on Tuesday, May 29, were shooting at them on Thursday, May 31.

Everything was working for Mao. If the hungry were fed, it relieved food shortages and minimized talk of uprisings. If the people were rejected—as his government had been told—it reinforced the Communists' "Hate the West" propaganda and harassed Hong Kong. The returning Chinese heard cadres announce over loudspeakers: "They are imperialists and they must be driven out of Hong Kong and Asia. This is colonialism."

This is what makes Hong Kong one of the world's most unique places today. It is indeed colonialism, and colonialism is supposed to be dead. It has represented such an embarrassing hangover from nineteenth-century colonialism that President Franklin Roosevelt twice asked Winston Churchill to persuade England to return Hong Kong to China.

Despite its pain and poverty—hunger stalking the streets and lean-tos against mansions—Hong Kong is such a portrait of prosperity in contrast to Communist China that it is an indictment against Mao Tse-tung's regime. There is no marked geographical distinction between Hong Kong and China. There is plenty of land on China's side; there is no land, unless it is carved from a mountain or reclaimed from the sea, on Hong Kong's side. Communist China was compelled to embarrass the colony.

Hong Kong can expect refugee explosions, harassment

and the continuing "problem of people" as long as China remains under its present type of Communist rule and as long as Hong Kong—a dot on the China map—remains a part of the free world. People have always searched out the bridge to freedom.

# INDEX

245